Great Lake Lighthouses

Jane Moorman

The Journey

Since my brother's Cub Scout Troop created the Great Lakes in our sandbox when we were kids, I've always wanted to see the largest group of fresh water lakes on Earth.

During a month-long road trip I drove from the Canada border in Minnesota to the St. Lawrence River along the United States coastline of each lake.

Before leaving on the trip I obtained a National Geographic map of the lakes. There were a few lighthouses marked on the map, so I thought, "I'll take photos of lighthouse during my journey."

Once on the road, I discovered a wonderful website lighthousefriends.com that provided directions to all of the lighthouses in each state. By the journey's end, I had photographed 101 lighthouses.

So buckle your seat belt and join me on this pictorial journey to some of the most interesting historical architecture. Don't worry it's not all 101, just the best ones.

Along the way I will share some of my adventures and insights.

Jane Moorman

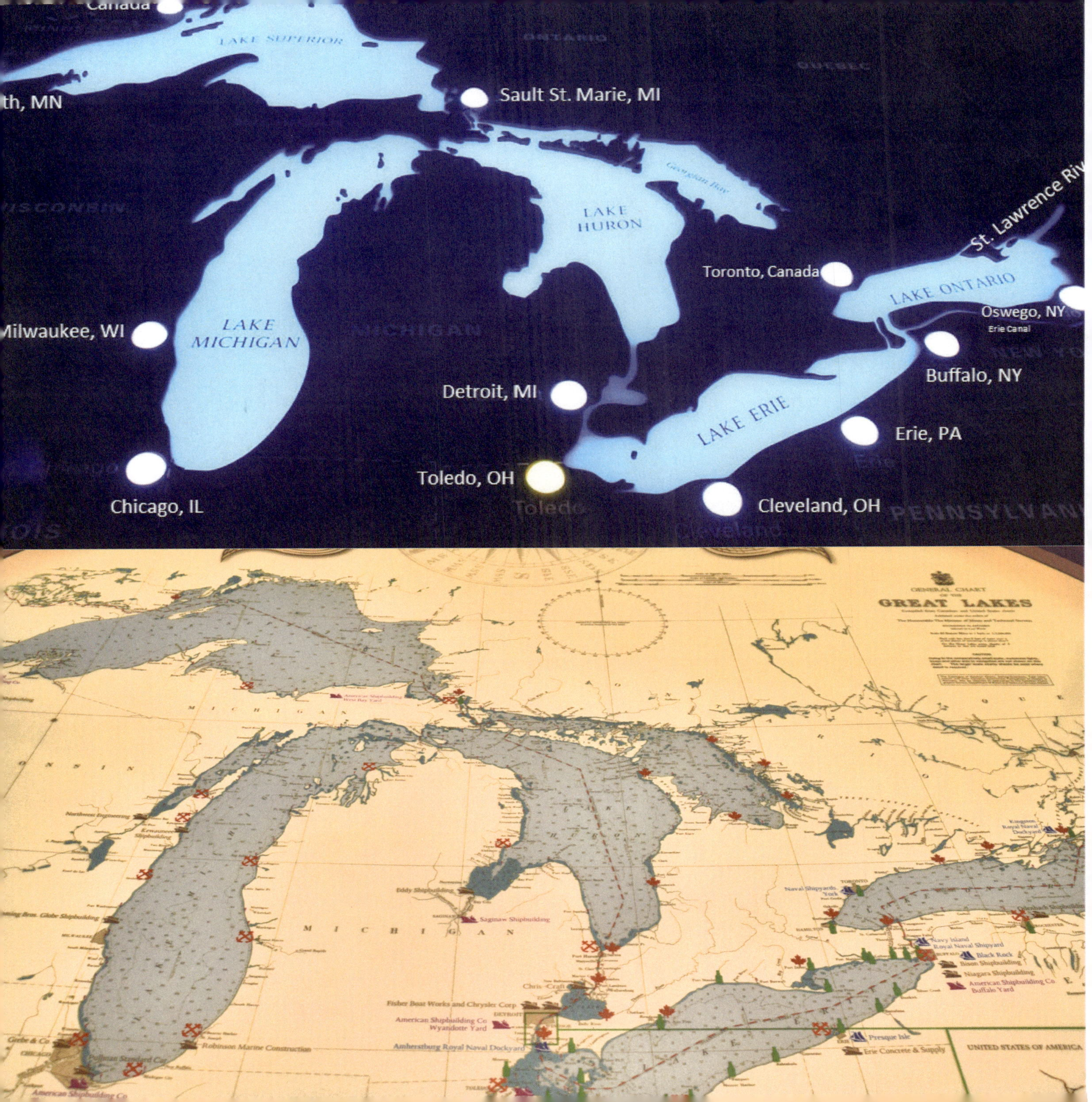

Canada
LAKE SUPERIOR
ONTARIO
QUEBEC
th, MN
Sault St. Marie, MI
WISCONSIN
Georgian Bay
LAKE HURON
St. Lawrence River
MICHIGAN
Toronto, Canada
LAKE ONTARIO
Milwaukee, WI
LAKE MICHIGAN
Oswego, NY
Erie Canal
NEW YORK
Buffalo, NY
Detroit, MI
LAKE ERIE
Erie, PA
Toledo, OH
Erie
Chicago, IL
Cleveland, OH
PENNSYLVANIA
ILLINOIS

GENERAL CHART
OF THE
GREAT LAKES
MICHIGAN
American Shipbuilding
West Bay Yard
Kingston
Royal Naval
Dockyard
Northwest Engineering
Kewaunee
Shipbuilding
Eddy Shipbuilding
MICHIGAN
Saginaw Shipbuilding
TORONTO
Naval Shipyards
York
WISCONSIN
Leathem Smith Globe Shipbuilding
Grand Rapids
Port Huron
HAMILTON
Navy Island
Royal Naval Shipyard
Black Rock
Boem Shipbuilding
Niagara Shipbuilding
American Shipbuilding
Buffalo Yard
Chris-Craft
Fisher Boat Works and Chrysler Corp
DETROIT
American Shipbuilding Co
Wyandotte Yard
Robinson Marine Construction
Amherstburg Royal Naval Dockyard
Presque Isle
Erie Concrete & Supply
UNITED STATES OF AMERICA
Grebe & Co
CHICAGO
American Shipbuilding Co
TOLEDO

Lake Superior

The indigenous Ojibwe people referred this lake as the great sea. It is the largest of the chain of lakes. Three states have shorelines along Lake Superior - Minnesota, Wisconsin and Michigan's Upper Peninsula.

Two areas of the rugged coastline are protected by the National Parks' Apostle Island National Lakeshore and Pictured Rocks National Lakeshore.

Most of the lighthouses are located on islands and are not viewable from the shore. I took two boat cruises to capture photos of three lighthouse and to see the beautiful rock formations carved by the lake water waves.

The tour at Split Rock Lighthouse State Park included climbing the tower to see the lamp globe rotate from underneath it.

Transportation of lumber and raw minerals from mining, as well as people, has been marred by 350 shipwrecks which caused the need for lighthouses and life saving rescue stations. Whitefish Point Light Station features the Great Lake Shipwreck Museum and a memorial to the SS Edmund Fitzgerald, the largest ship on the Great Lakes that sunk in 1975.

The SOO Locks at Sault St. Marie, MI, raises ships traveling from Lake Huron. I watched the process for one ship, then saw it at Point Iroquois and Whitefish Point a total of 42 nautical miles.

Split Rock Lighthouse
Split Rock State Park, Minnesota

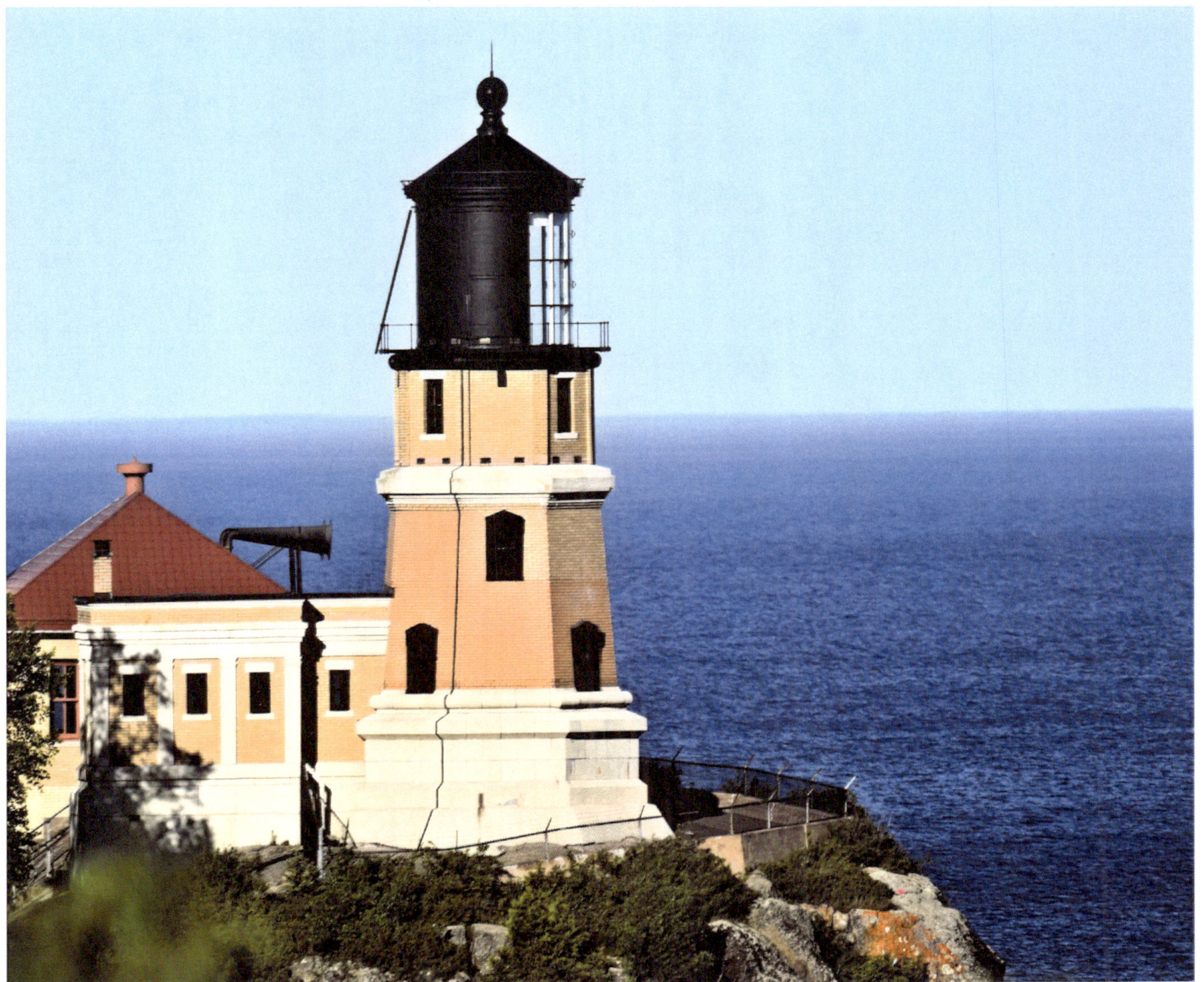

Constructed: 1909-1910 - First Light Exhibited: July 31, 1910 - Height: 54 feet

Decommissioned: January 1969 - Transferred to State of Minnesota: March 1971

Operator: Minnesota Historical Society 1976 - National Historic Landmark: 2011

Two Harbors, MN, Lighthouse

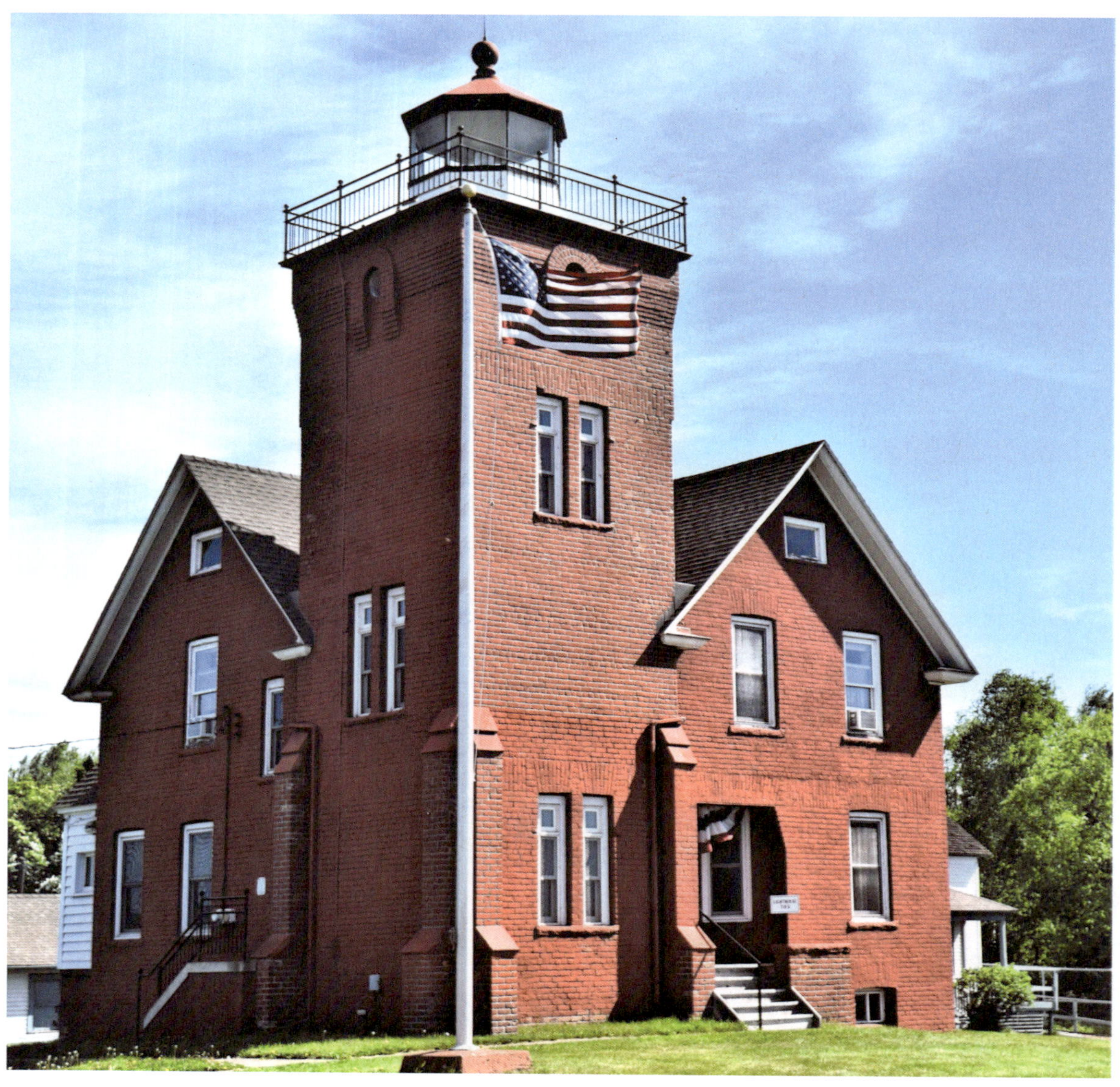

Constructed: November 1891 - First Light Exhibited: April 1892 - Height: 43.5 feet

Duluth, MN, South Harbor Breakwater Outer Lighthouse

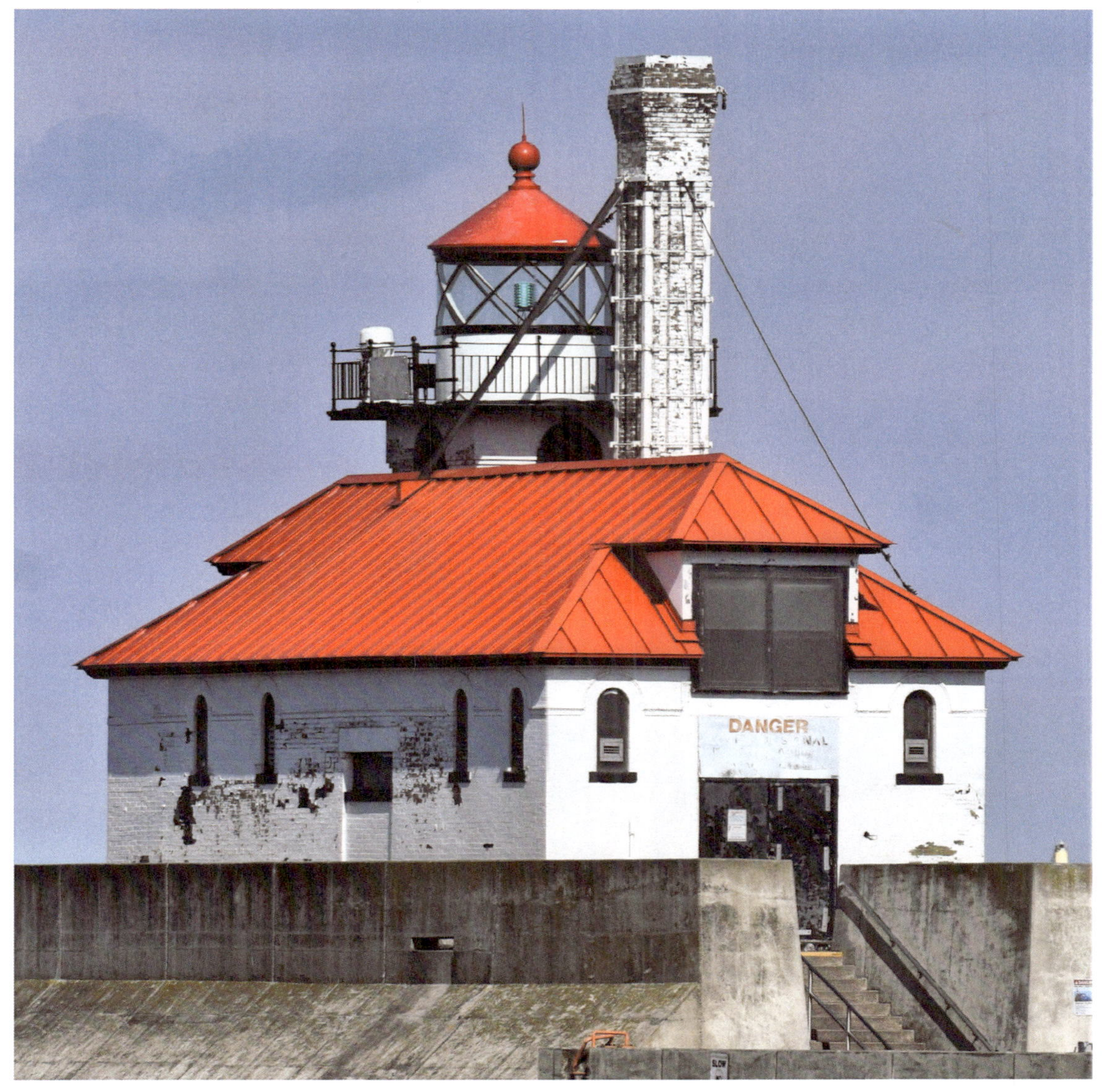

Constructed: January 1874 - First Light Exhibited: June 1874 - Height: 50 feet above lake level

National Register of Historic Places: 2016

Duluth, MN, North Breakwater Outer Lighthouse

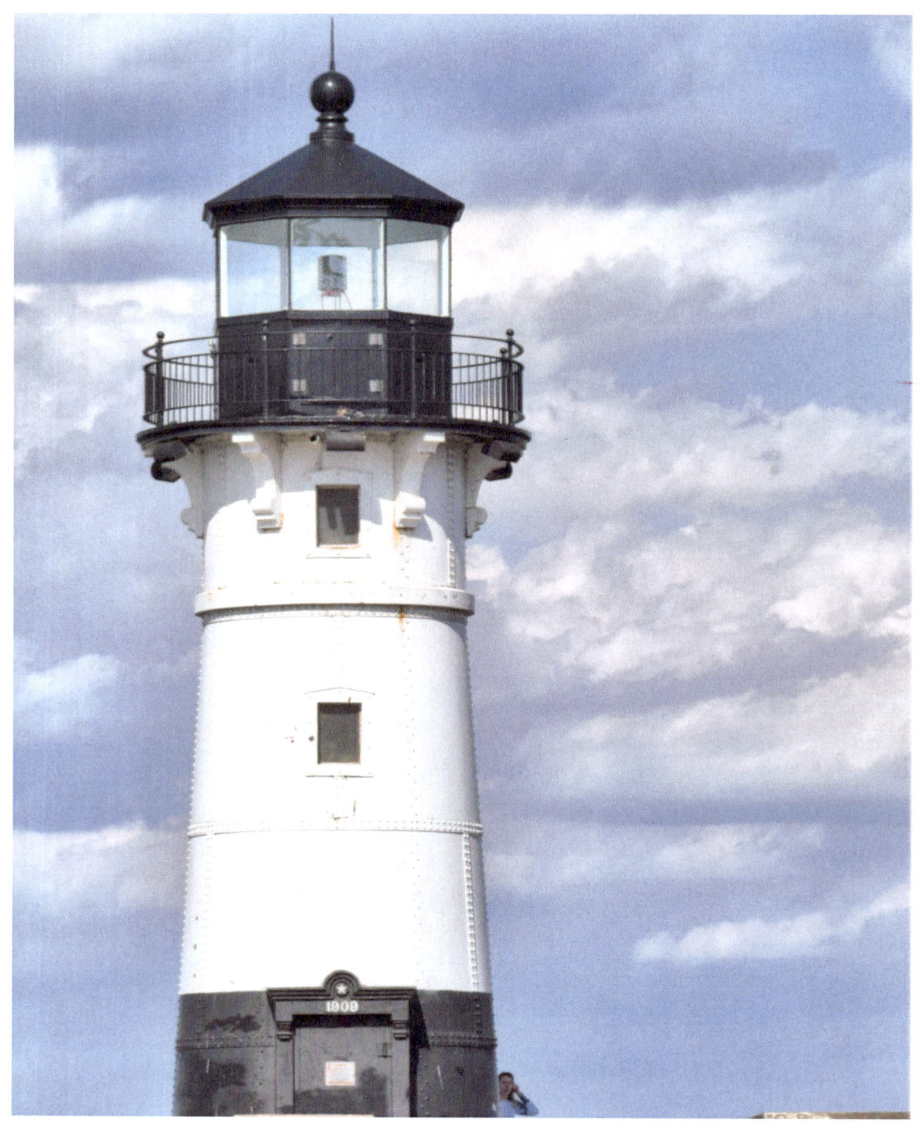

Constructed: 1909 - First Light Exhibited: April 1910 - Height: 50 feet above lake level

National Register of Historic Places: 2016

Raspberry Island Lighthouse
Apostle Islands National Lakeshore, Wisconsin

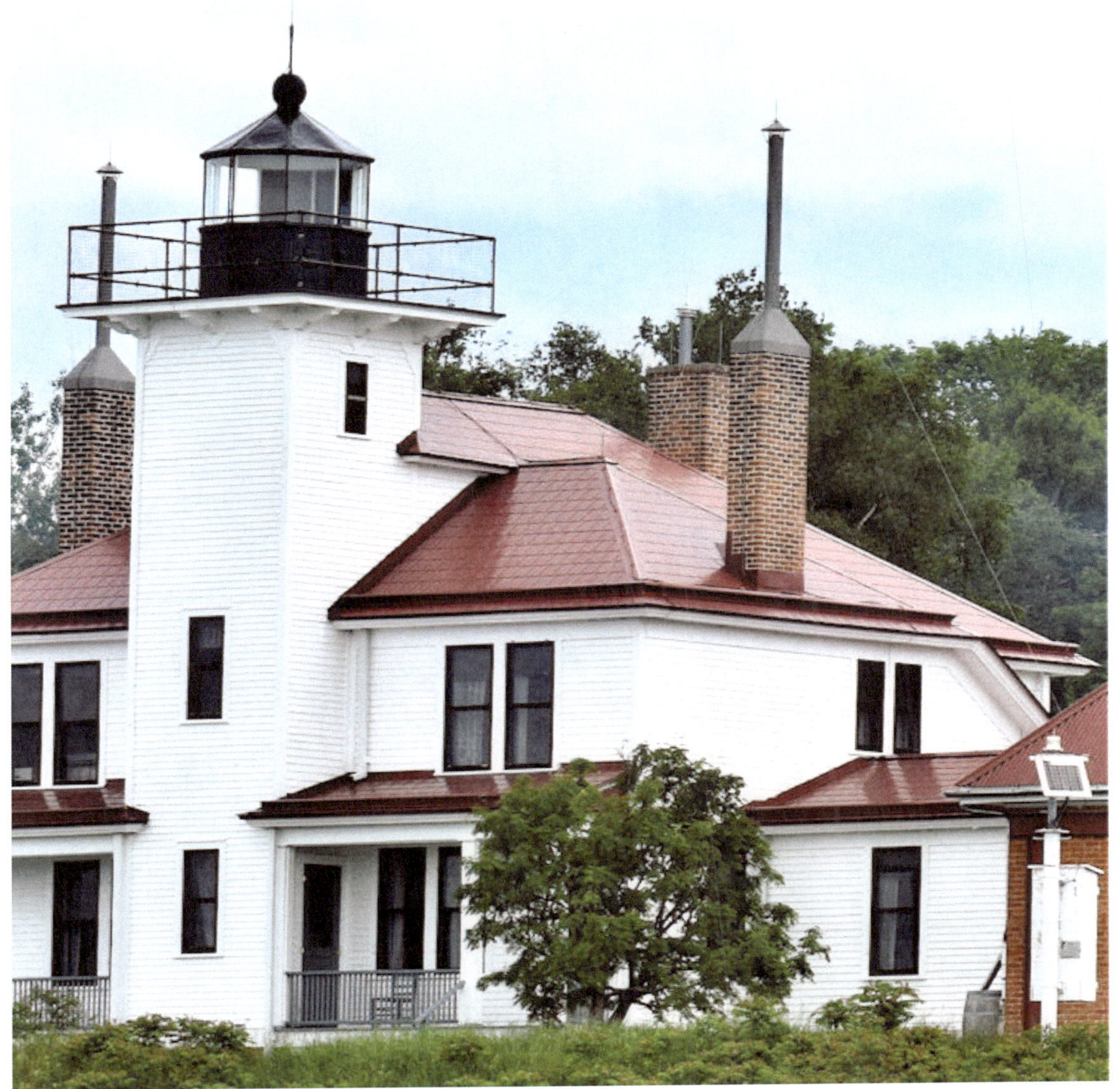

Constructed: 1862 - First Light Exhibited: July 1863

Owner: National Park Service: 1974 - Restored: 2002-2003 - Reopened to pubic: 2007

Sand Island Lighthouse

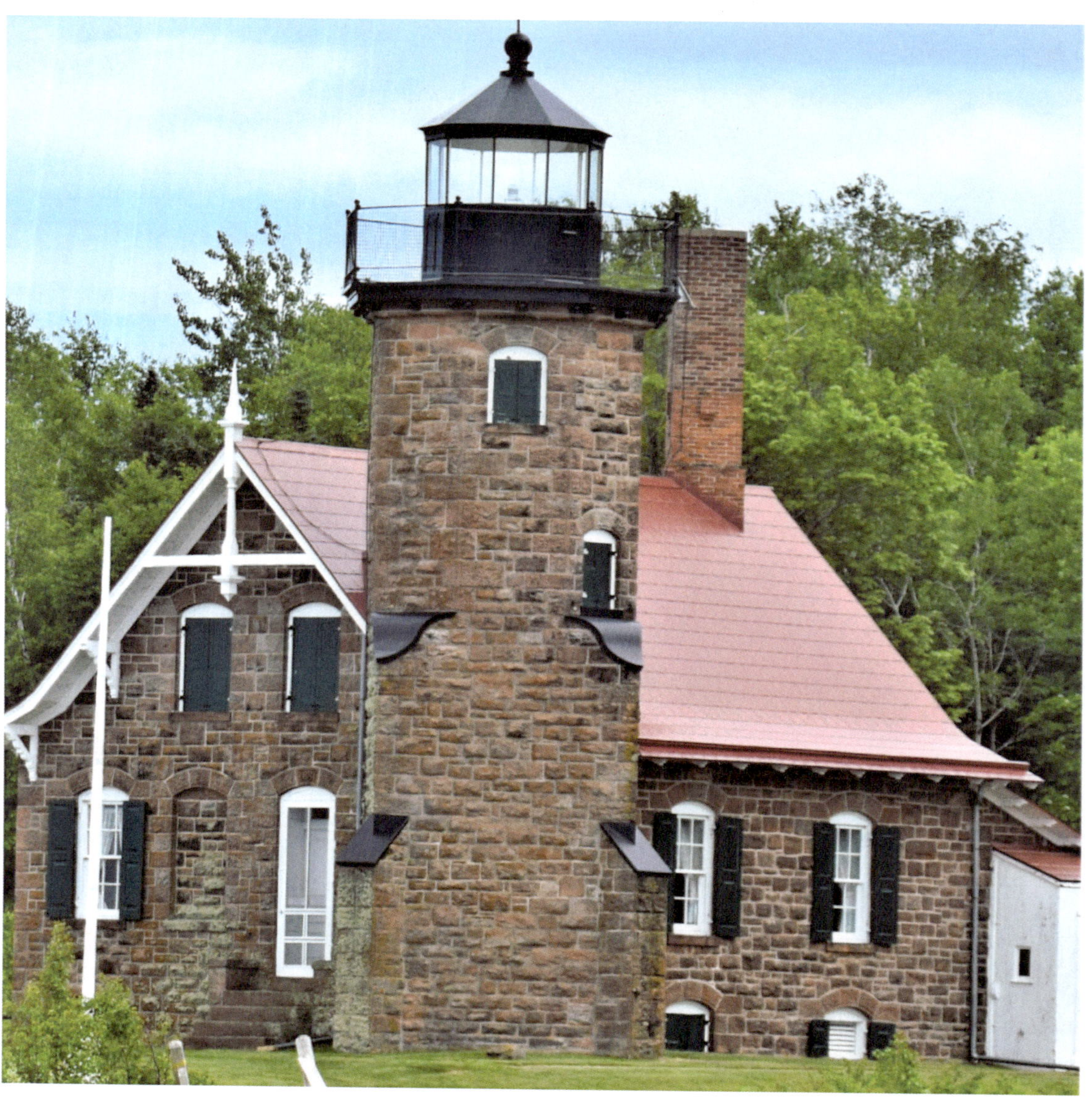

Constructed: 1880 - Norman Gothic design of sandstone - First Light Exhibited: September 1881 - Height: 42 feet Apostle Islands National Lakeshore, National Park Service: 1974

Eagle Harbor Lighthouse
Eagle Harbor, Michigan Upper Peninsula

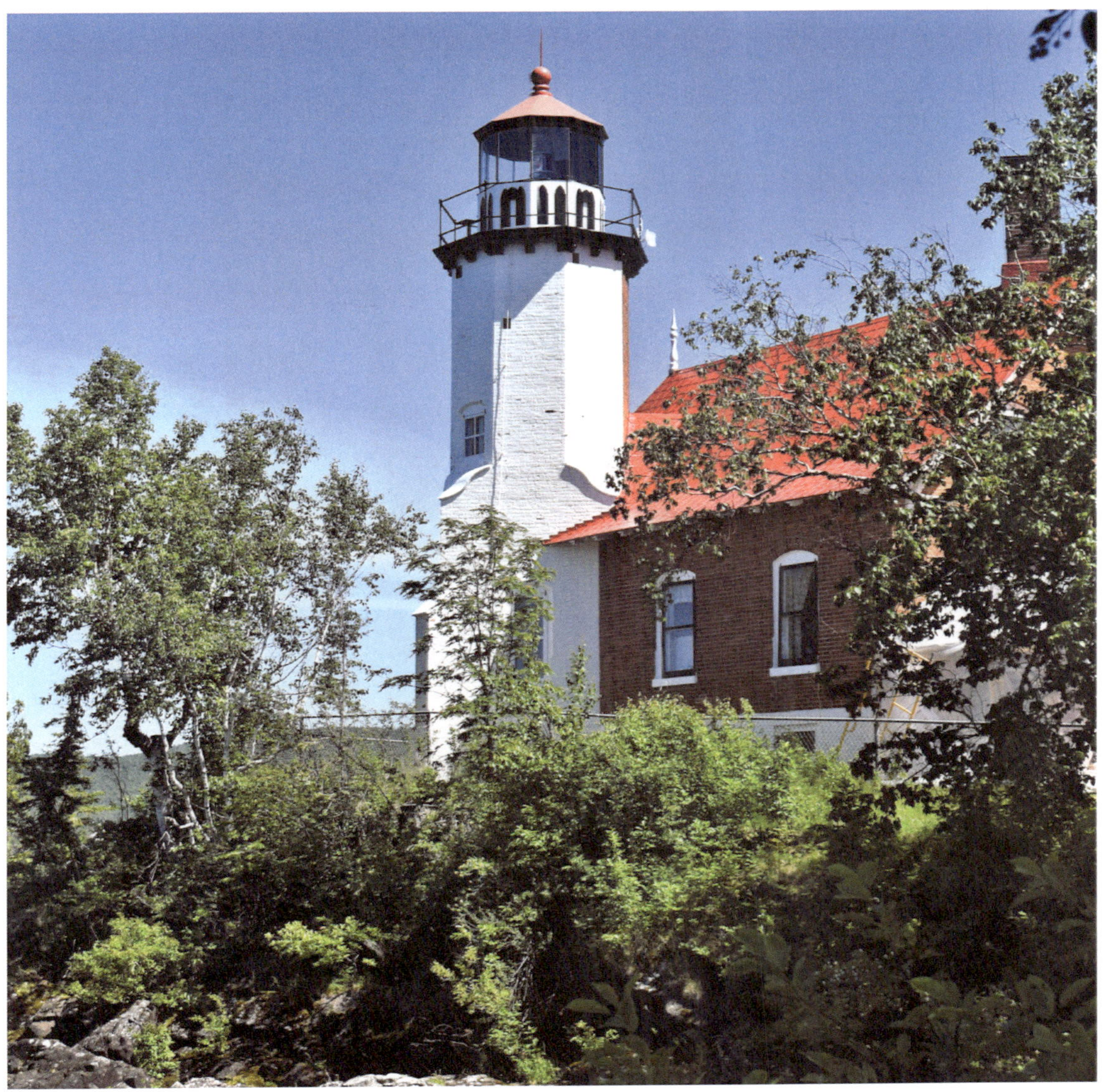

Constructed: 1871 - Norman Gothic Style Lighthouse - Original Light Exhibited: 1850
Tower made more visible in daylight by painting lake side white
Current Owner: Keweenaw County Historical Society: stewardship 1982, full ownership 1991

Copper Harbor Lighthouse
Copper Harbor, Michigan Upper Peninsula

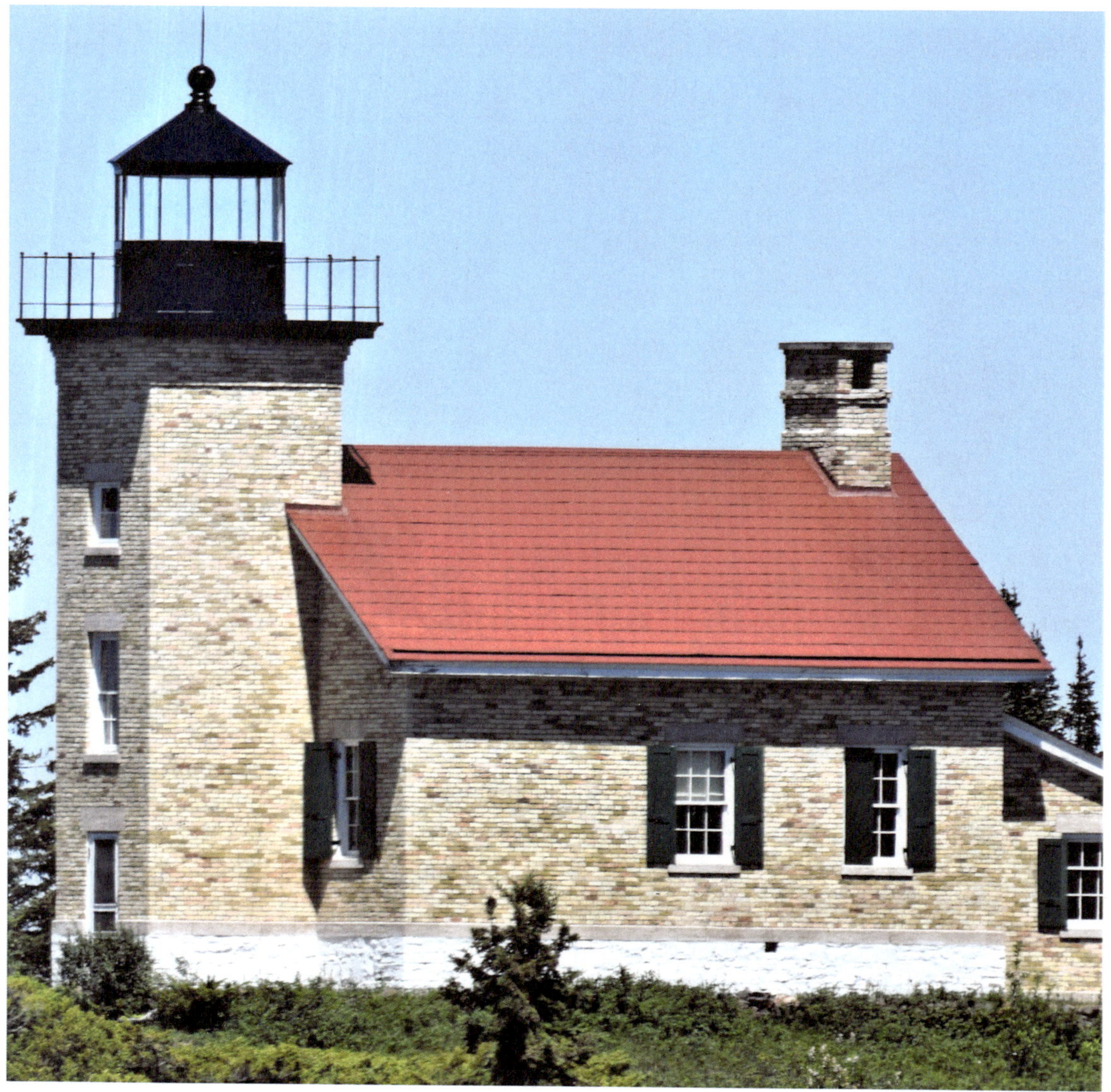

Constructed: 1848 - First Light Exhibited: Spring 1849 - Height 44 feet

Sold to State of Michigan by US Coast Guard: 1958

Michigan State Park Service opened to visitors: August 1975

Mendota Lighthouse - Bete Grise Bay

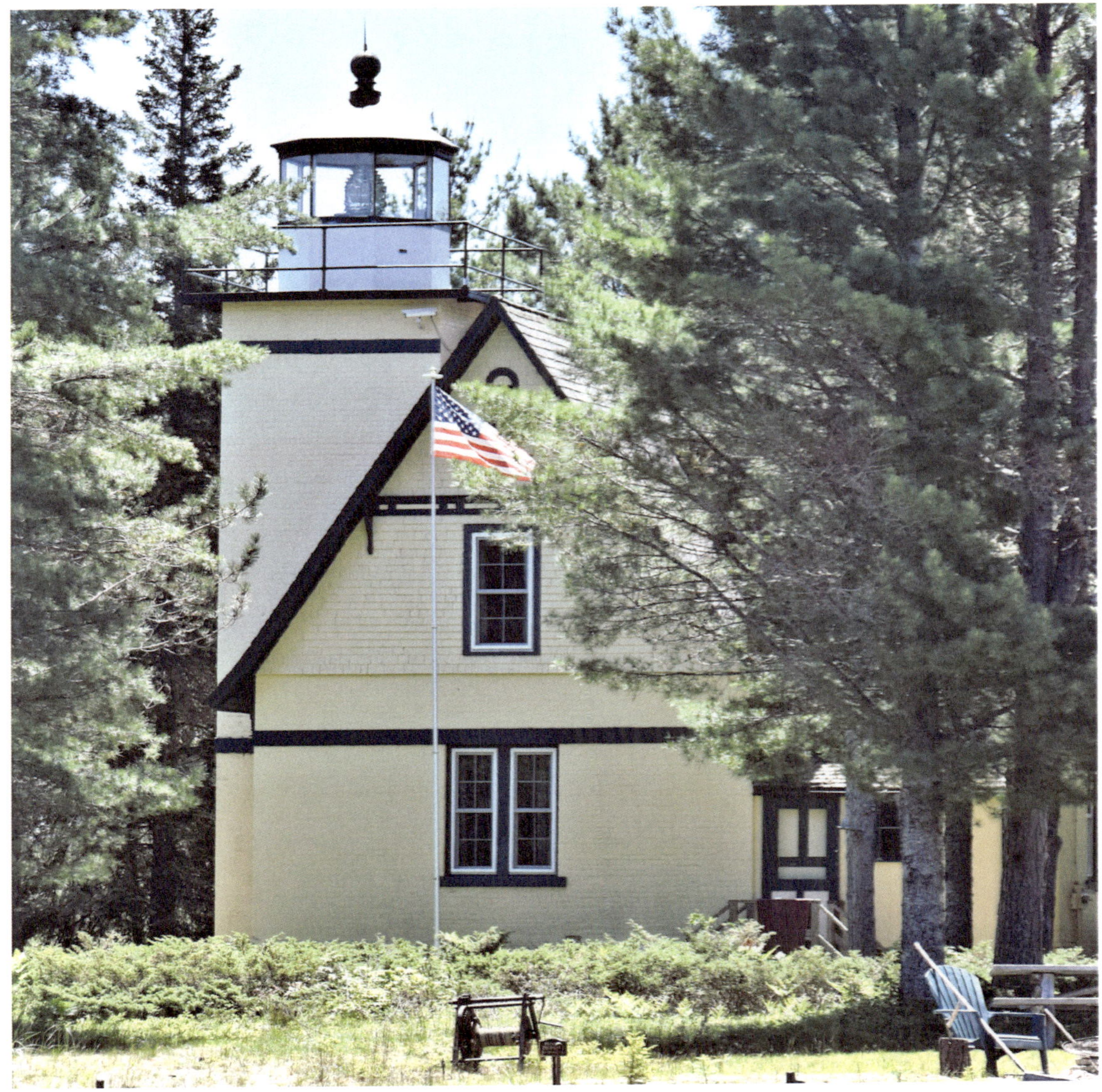

Constructed: 1895 - First Light Exhibited: November 1895

Unique: Tower centered on house longer wall - First privately owned by Gary Kohs 1997

Sand Point Lighthouse at Baraga, MI

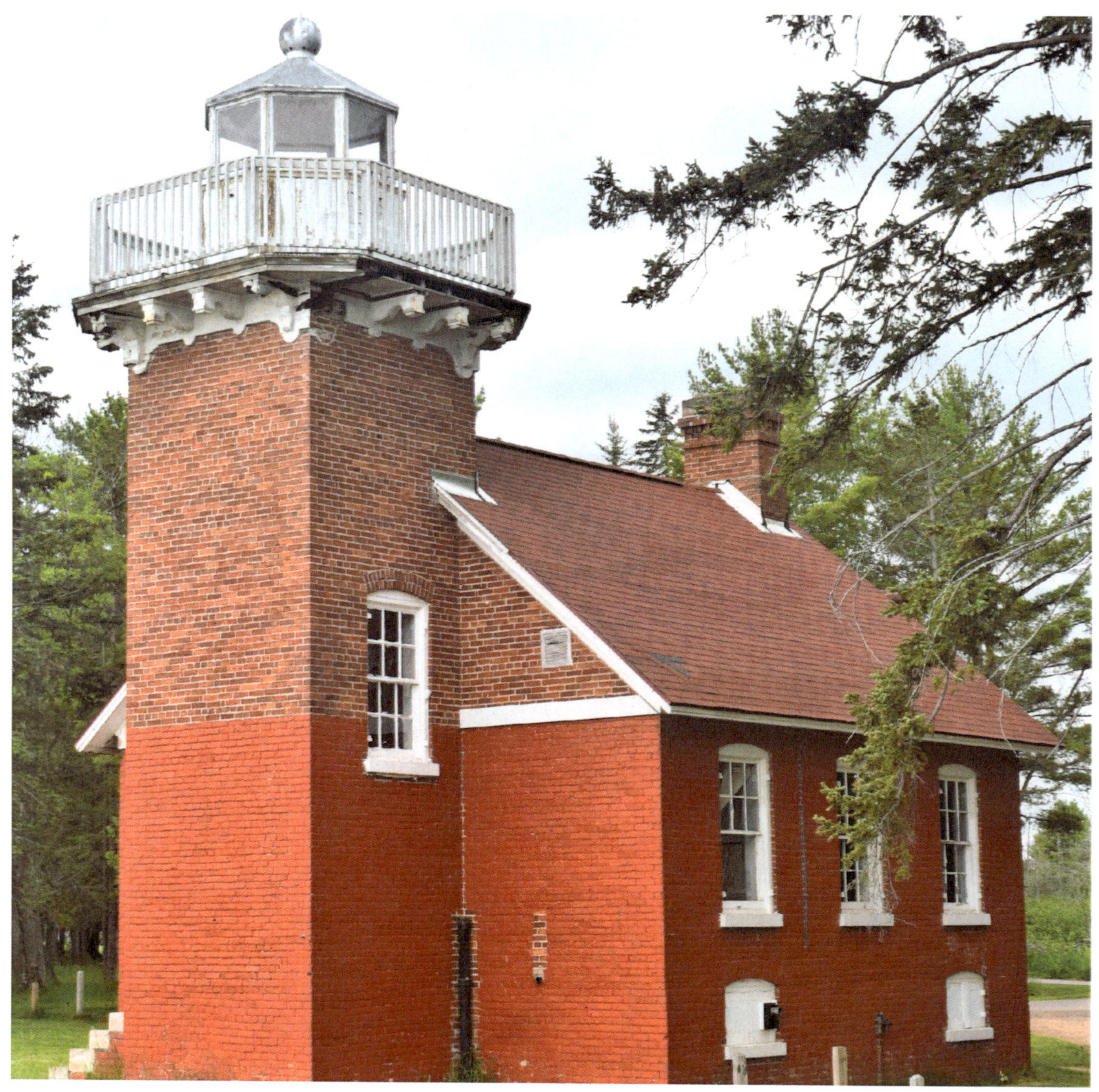

Constructed: 1877 - First Light Exhibited: August 1878 - Height: 36.5 feet

Keweenaw Bay Indian Community purchased in 1994

Munising, MI, Range Lighthouse

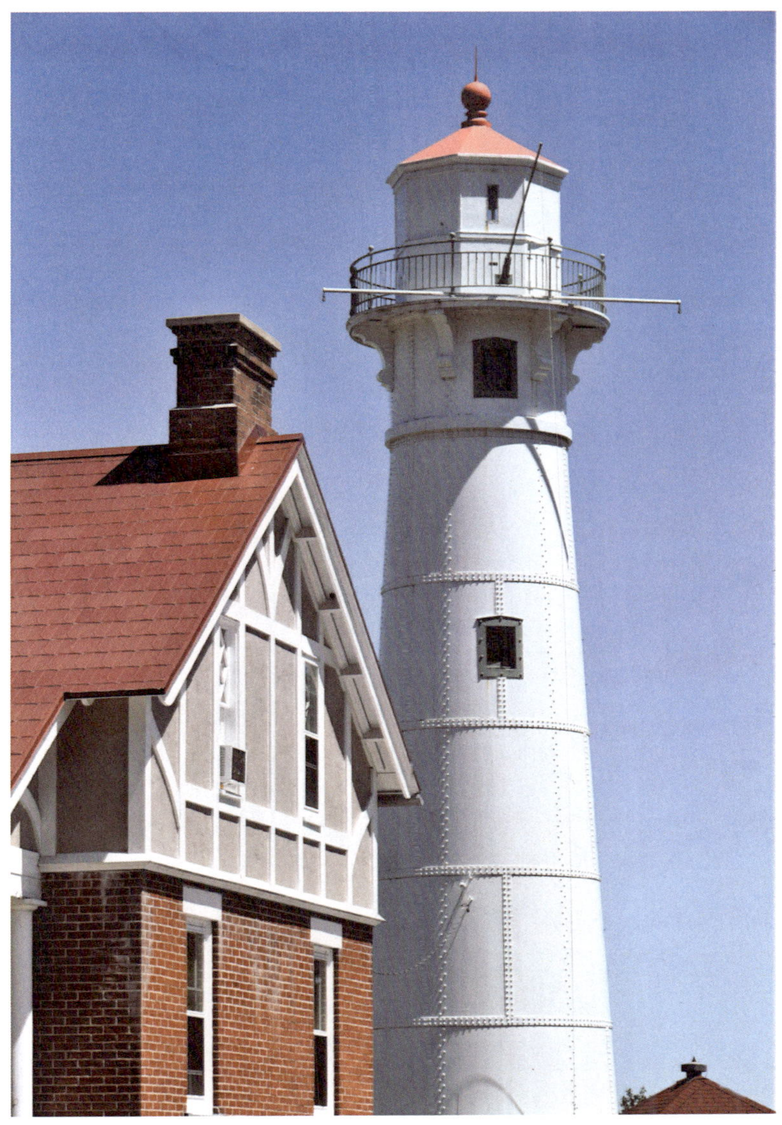

Constructed: 1908 - First Light Exhibited: October 1908 - Height: 31 feet

Ownership: US National Parks Pictured Rocks National Lakeshore July 2002

Grand Island East Channel Lighthouse
Pictured Rocks National Lakeshore

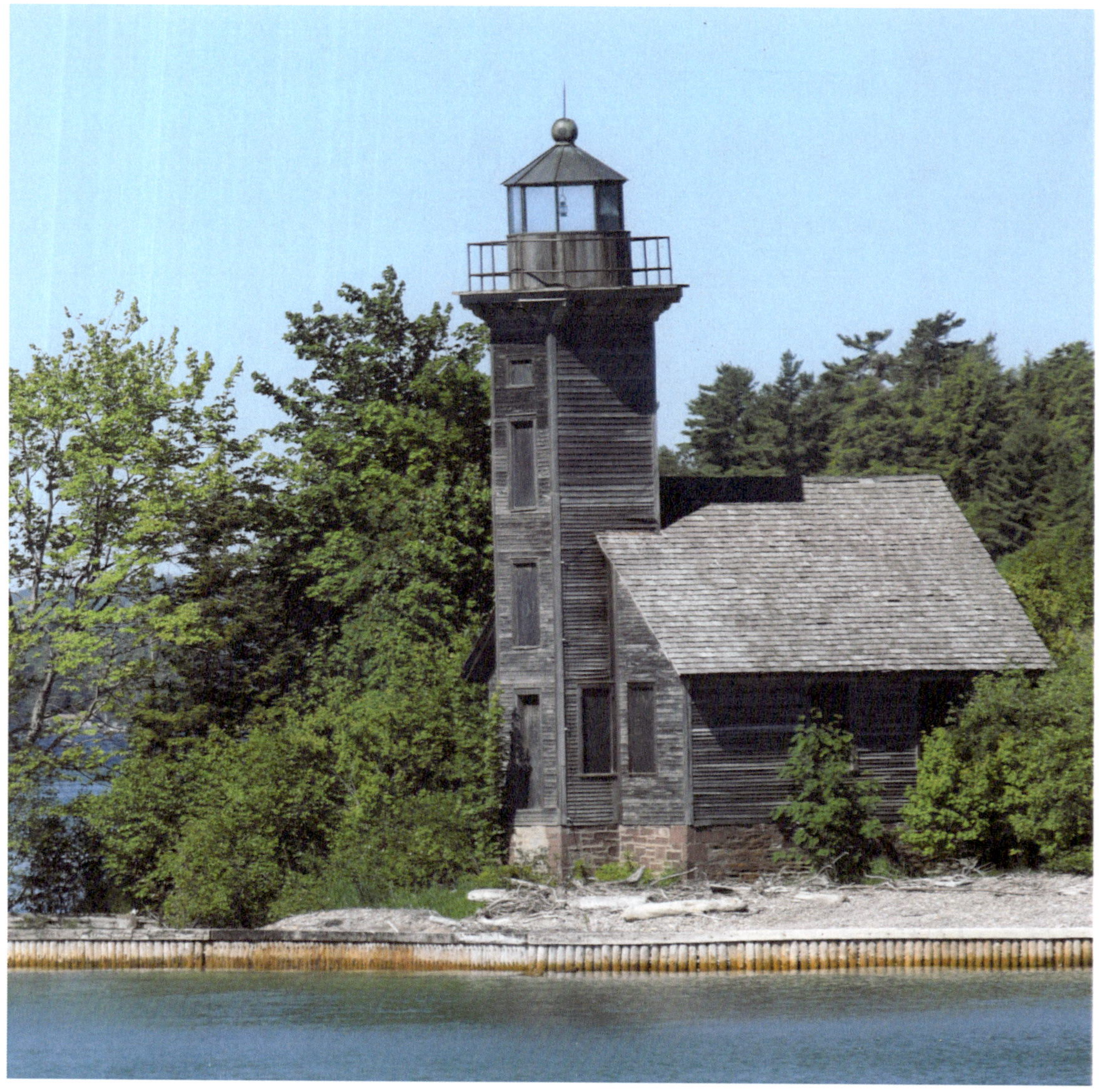

Constructed: 1868 - First Light Exhibited: August 1868 - Height: 41 feet
Cedar Wood Siding Structure - Decommissioned: 1905
First Private Owners: Munising Moose Lodge 1913
1999 Alger County Historical Society formed East Channel Lighthouse Rescue Committee

Au Sable Point Lighthouse - Pictured Rocks National Lakeshore

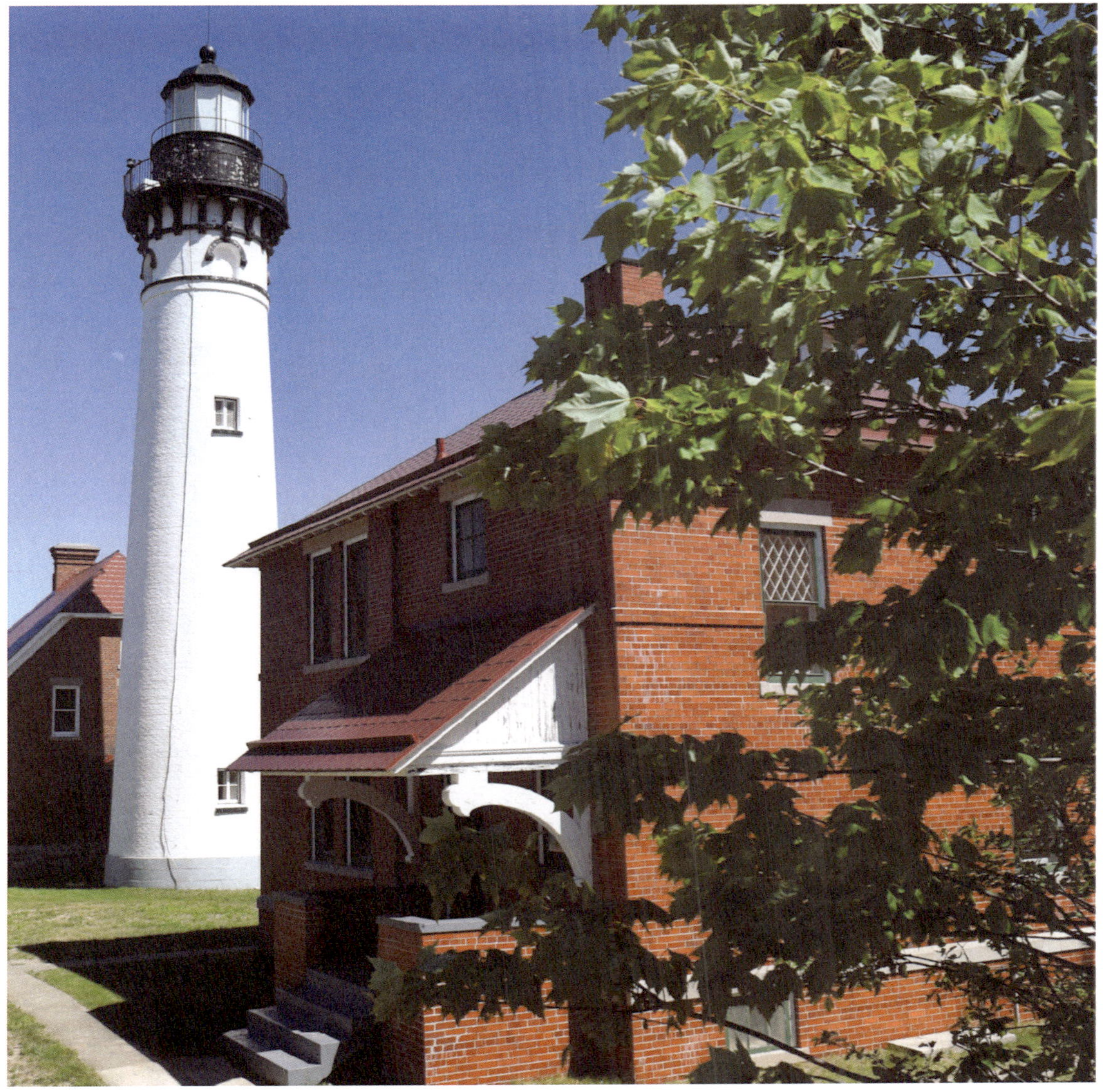

Constructed: 1873 - First Light Exhibited: August 1874 - Height: 86 feet

Whitefish Point Lighthouse, Michigan Upper Penisula

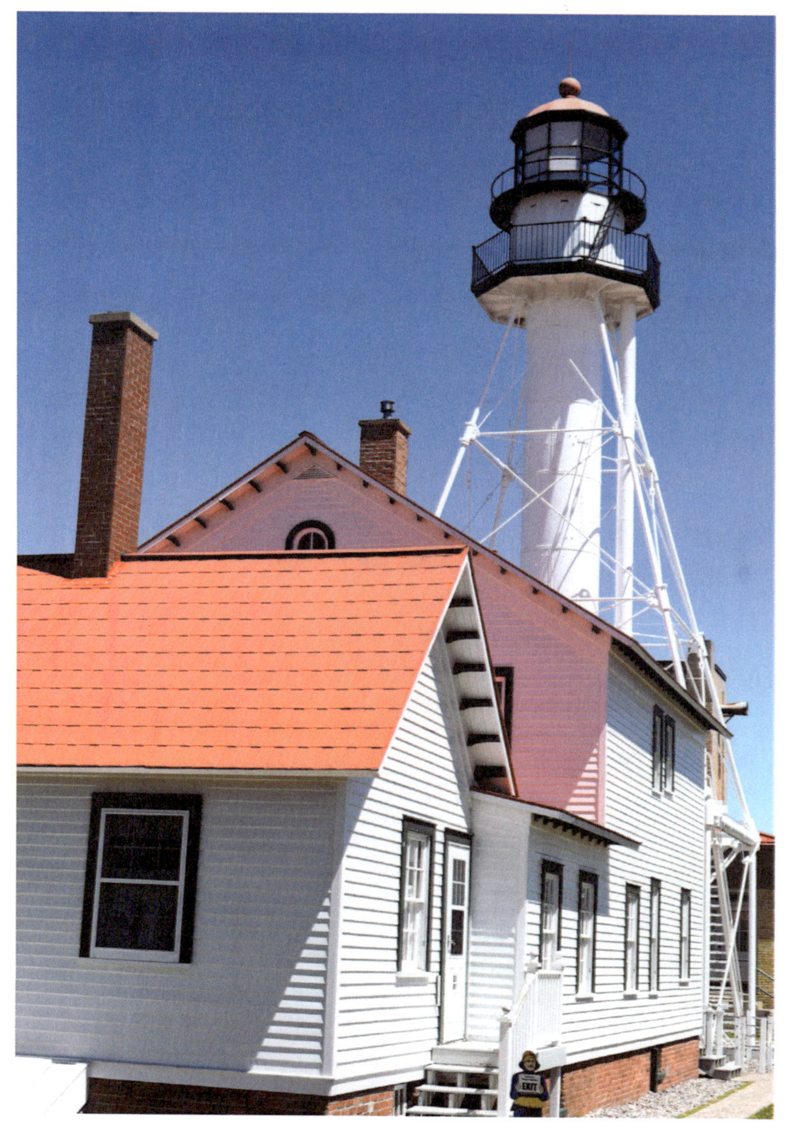

Constructed: Original Tower 1848 - 76-foot Metal Tower 1861 - First Light Exhibited : Spring 1858

US Coast Guard Rescue Station 1922-1951 - Great Lakes Shipwreck Historical Society lease: 1985

Point Iroqupis Lighthouse - Michigan Upper Penisula

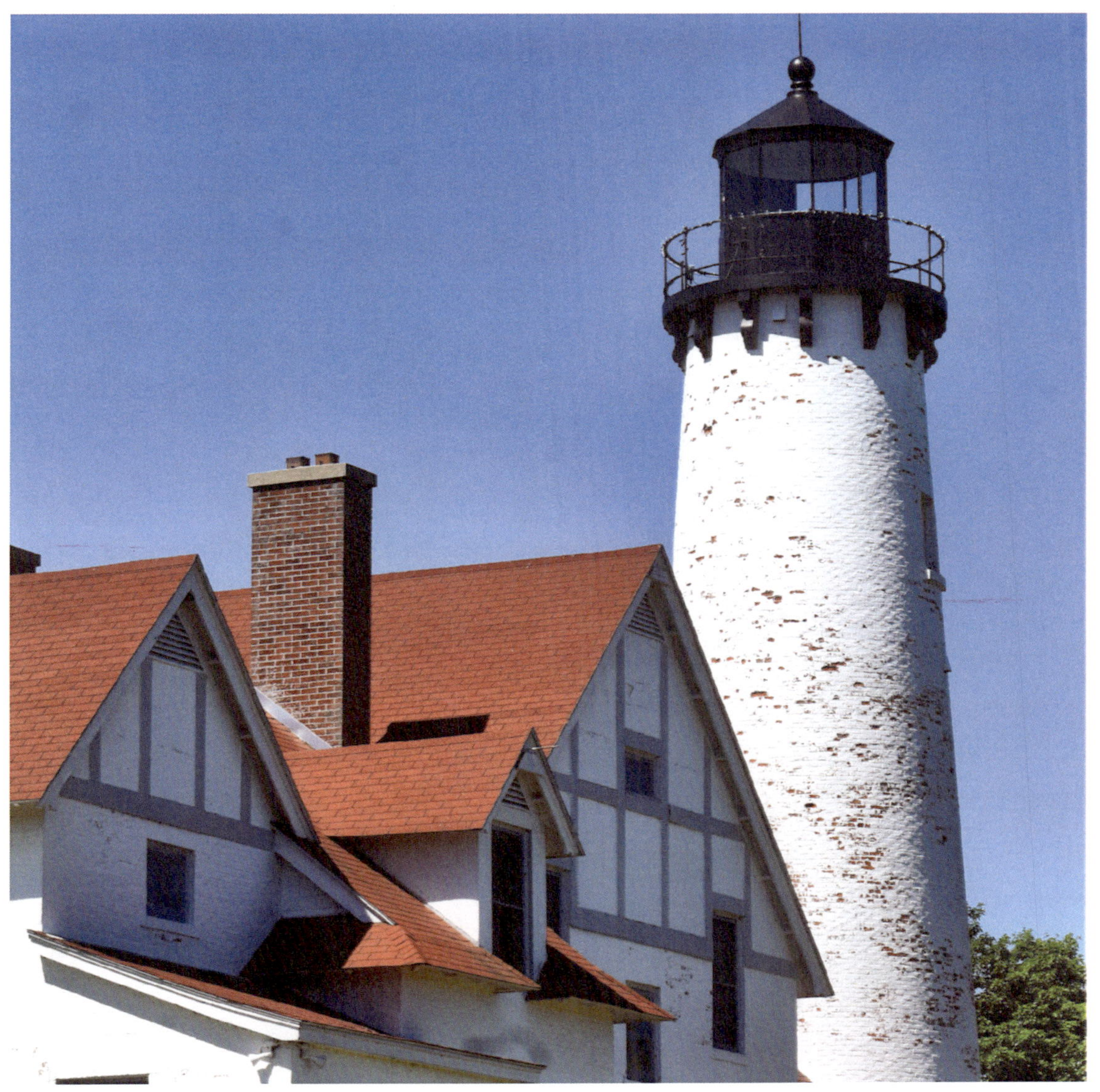

Constructed: Original Tower 1855, Existing 62-foot Tower 1870 - First Light Exhibited: 1856

Lake Michigan

Lake Michigan is the only Great Lake completely in the United States. So I visited 39 lighthouses long its shorelines, more than along the other lakes.

On this journey, we traveled west along the northern end of the lake, then south along its west side to Chicago before heading north on the east side back to Mackinaw City.

The architectural design and materials used to build the lighthouses varied.

One common design is the Norman Gothic style - notable by its square tower that has its corners beveled to create an octagonal form about midway up the tower. Several of the dwellings' chimney are set diagonal to the roof apex.

Another common design was dwelling roofs depicting a sail boat with the roof flaring out at the bottom. Masts are depicted at the gable end of the roof. Eagle Bluff Lighthouse is a good example. Seul Choix Point is unique with the bowed ends depicting sails.

Pottawatomie Lighthouse on Rock Island, off the Wisconsin's Door Peninsula between Green Bay and Lake Michigan, was the first lighthouse built on the Great Lakes. I had to ride two ferries and hike three miles to take this photo.

Another interesting tidbit is that the Kewaunee Pierhead Lighthouse and Holland Harbor Lighthouse on opposite sides of the lake are identical design. It was foggy when I was in Holland.

Seul Choix Point Lighthouse - Gulliver, MI

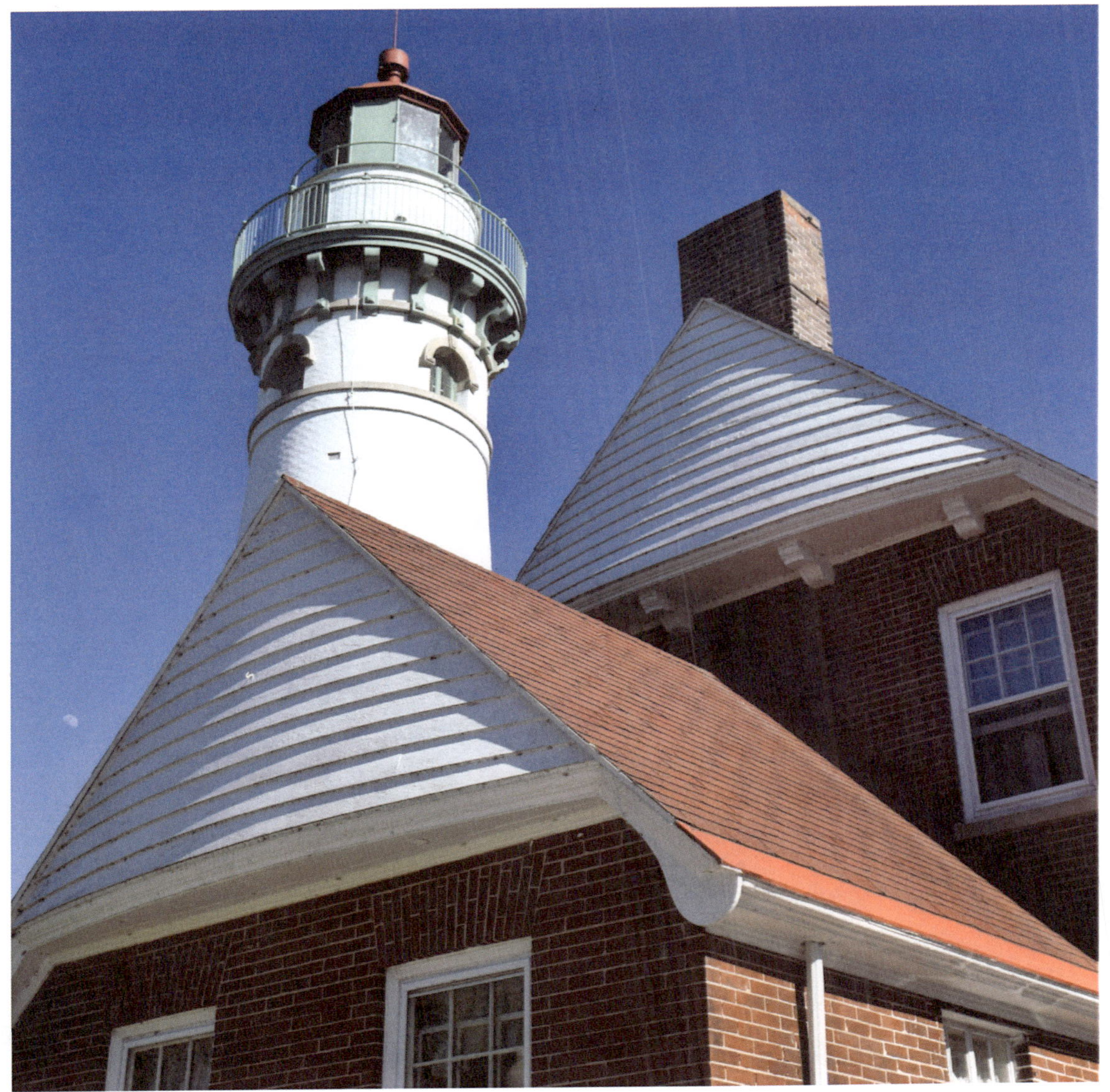

Many of the lightkeeper's house have designs that reflect sailboats. This one is unique because of it's 'sails.'

Constructed: 1892 - First Light Exhibited: 1895 - Height: 78 feet, 9 inches

Owner: Michigan Department of Natural Resources 1973

Gulliver Historical Society opened museum in 1987

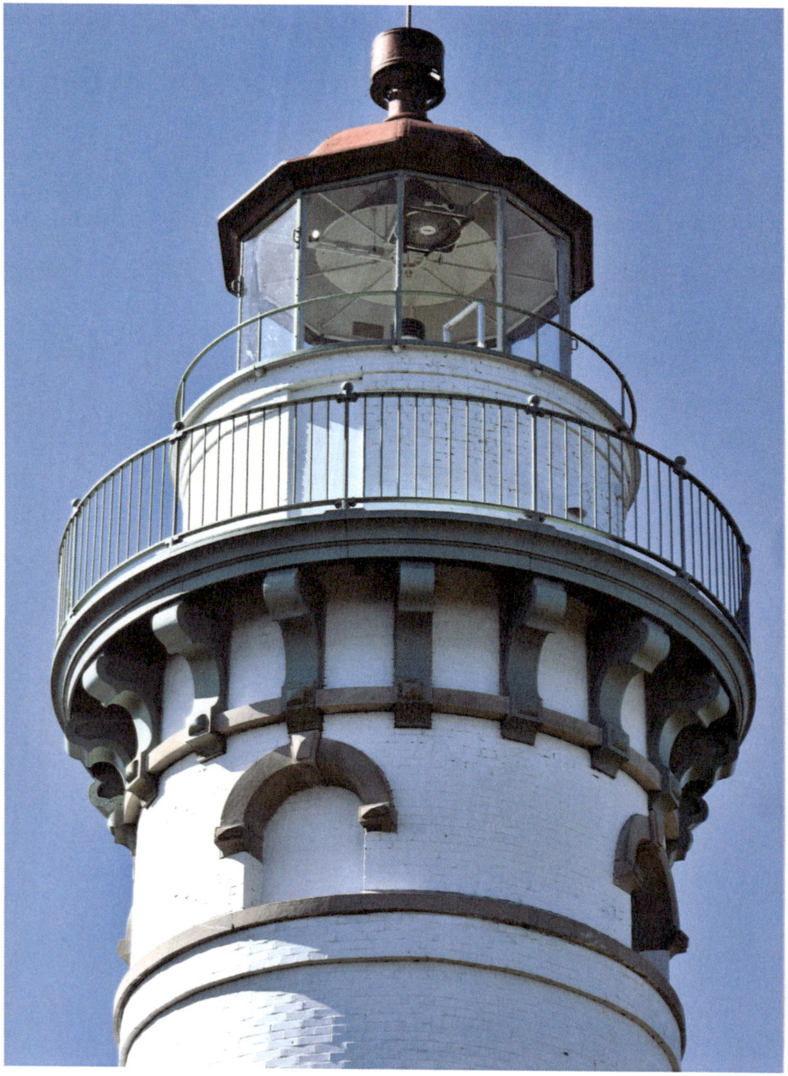

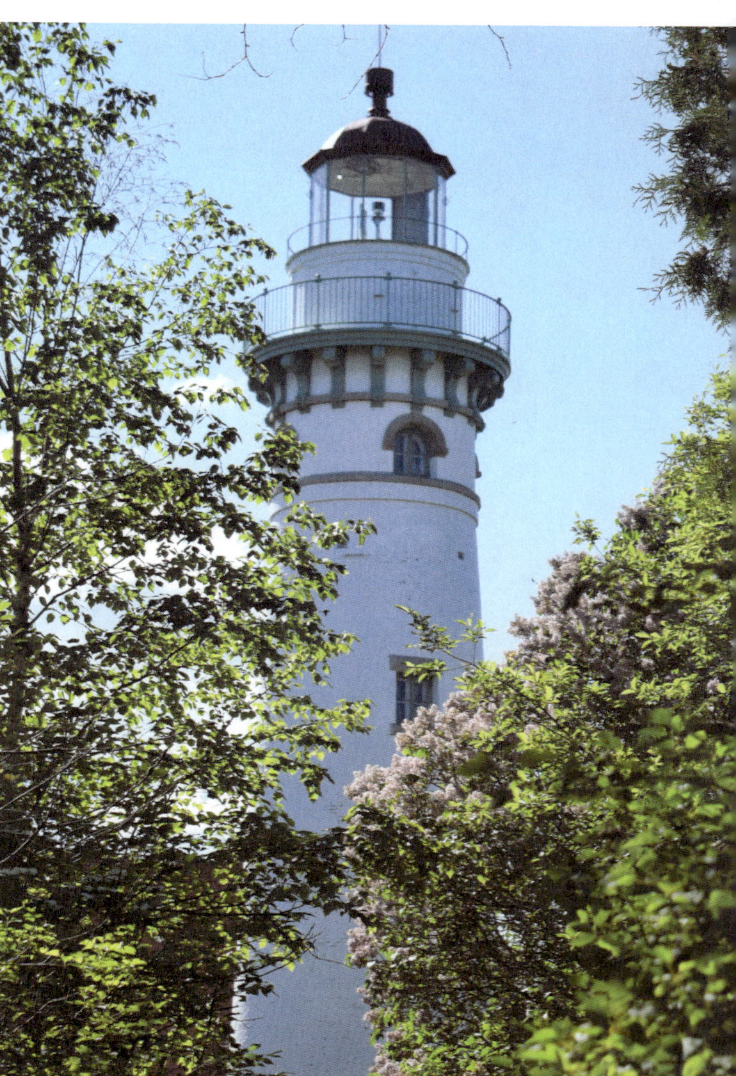

Sand Point Lighthouse, Escanaba, MI Upper Peninsula

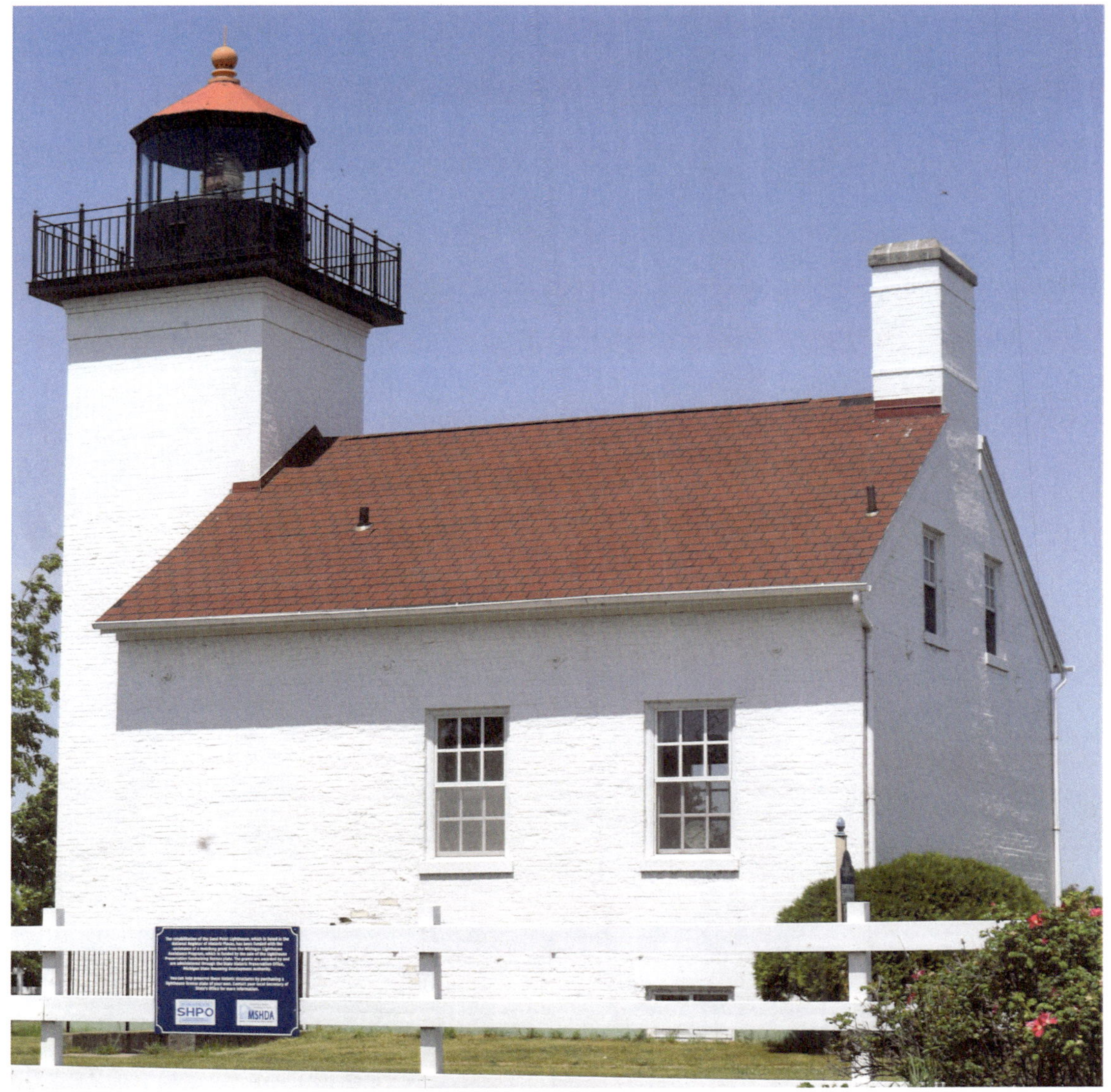

Constructed: 1867 - First Light Exhibited: May 1868 - Decommissioned: 1985 - Height: 44 feet above water surface

Current Owner: Delta County Historical Society since 1998

Sherwood Point Lighthouse, Idlewild, WI

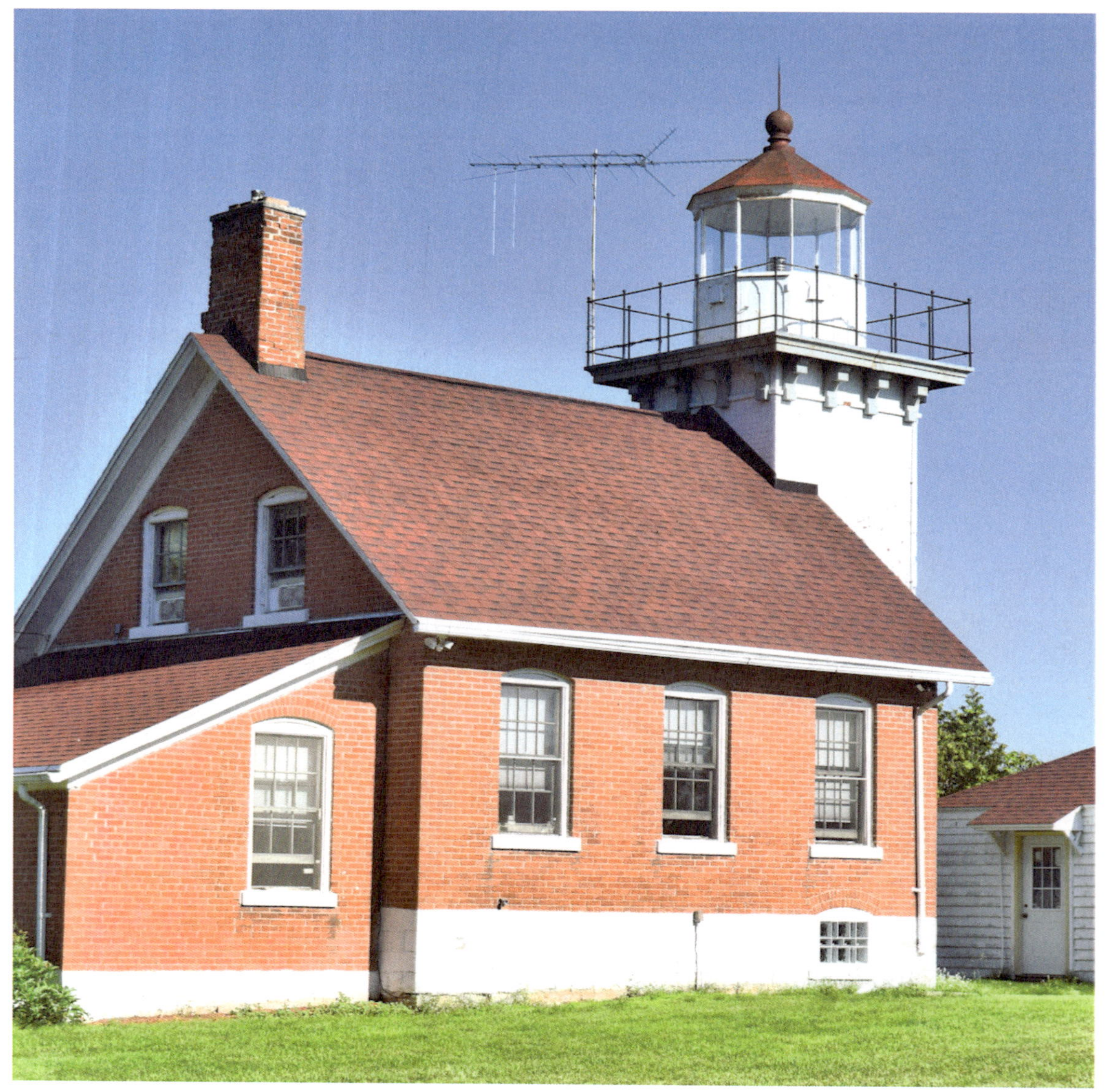

Constructed: 1883 - First Light Exhibited: October 1883 - Height: 36.5 feet
This was the last manned lighthouse on the Great Lakes when it became automated in 1983.
US Coast Guard continues to maintain the lighthouse and grounds.

Eagle Bluff Lighthouse - Door County, Wisconsin

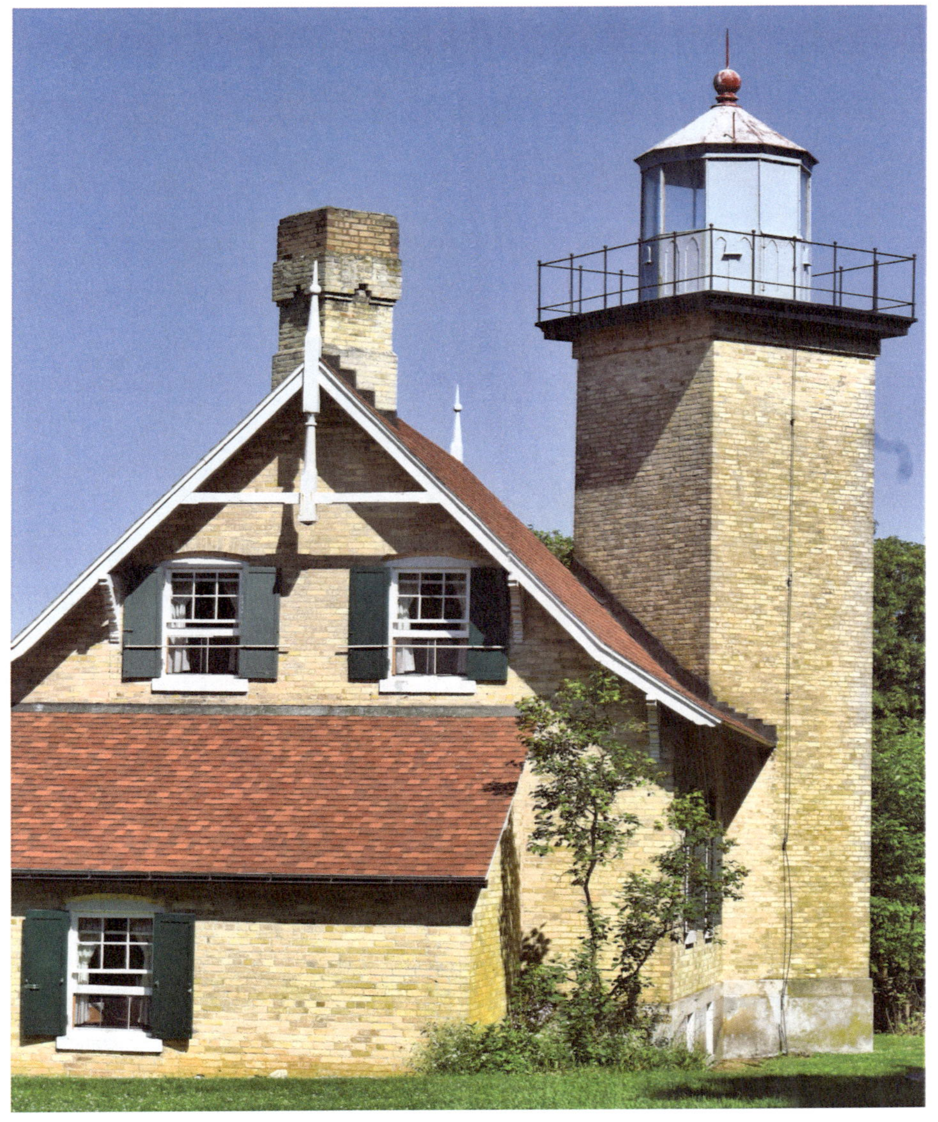

Constructed: 1868 - First Light Exhibited: October 1868 - Height: 36 feet

Unique angle of tower and chimney on this design that depicts a sail boat mast at the roofs apex.

Pottawatomie Lighthouse on Rock Island

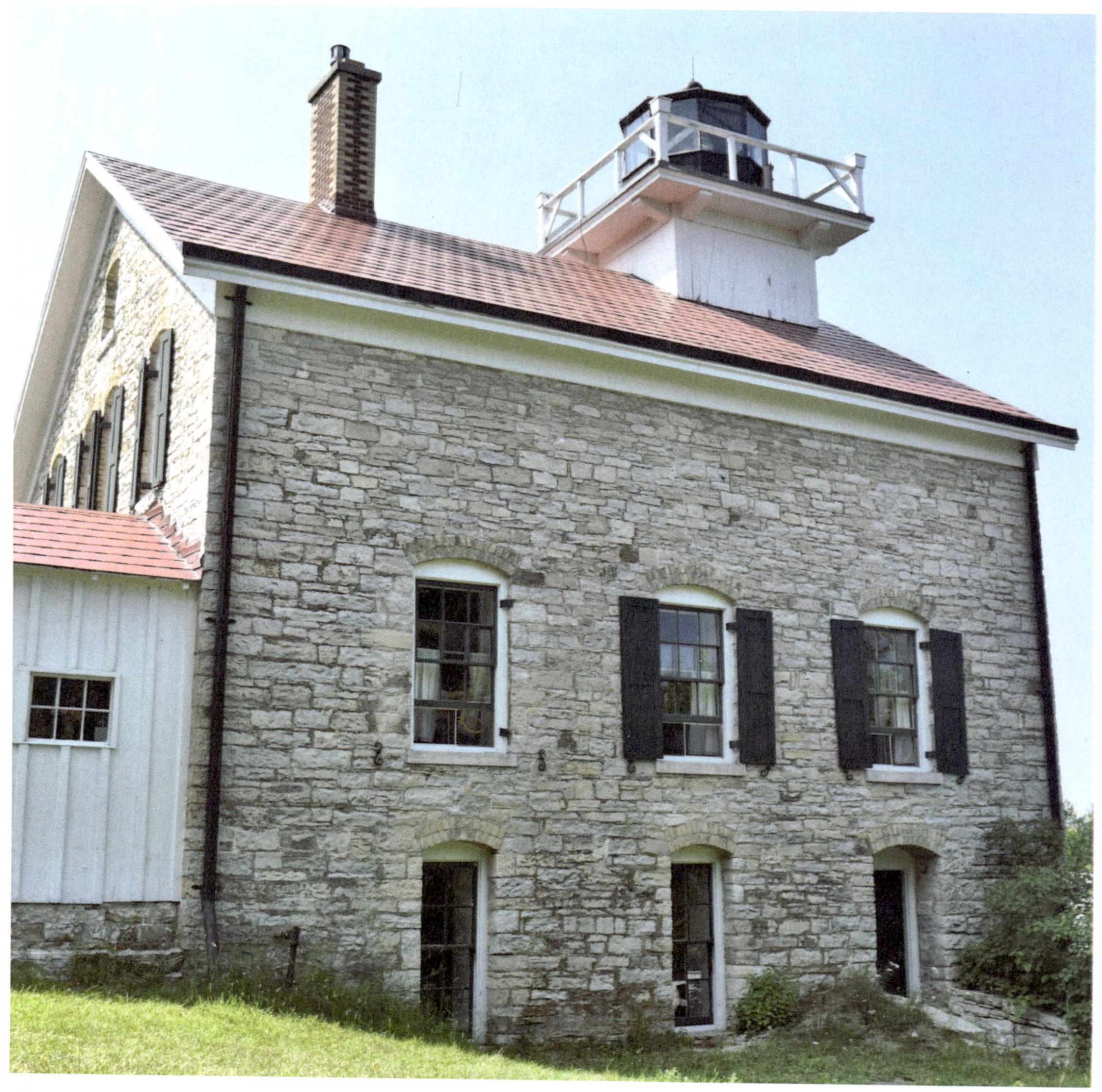

Constructed: Current structure 1858 - First Light Exhibited: 1859

Unique location of tower on roof of dwelling - Site of the first lighthouse on Great Lakes

Sturgeon Bay Ship Canal Lighthouse - Sturgeon, WI

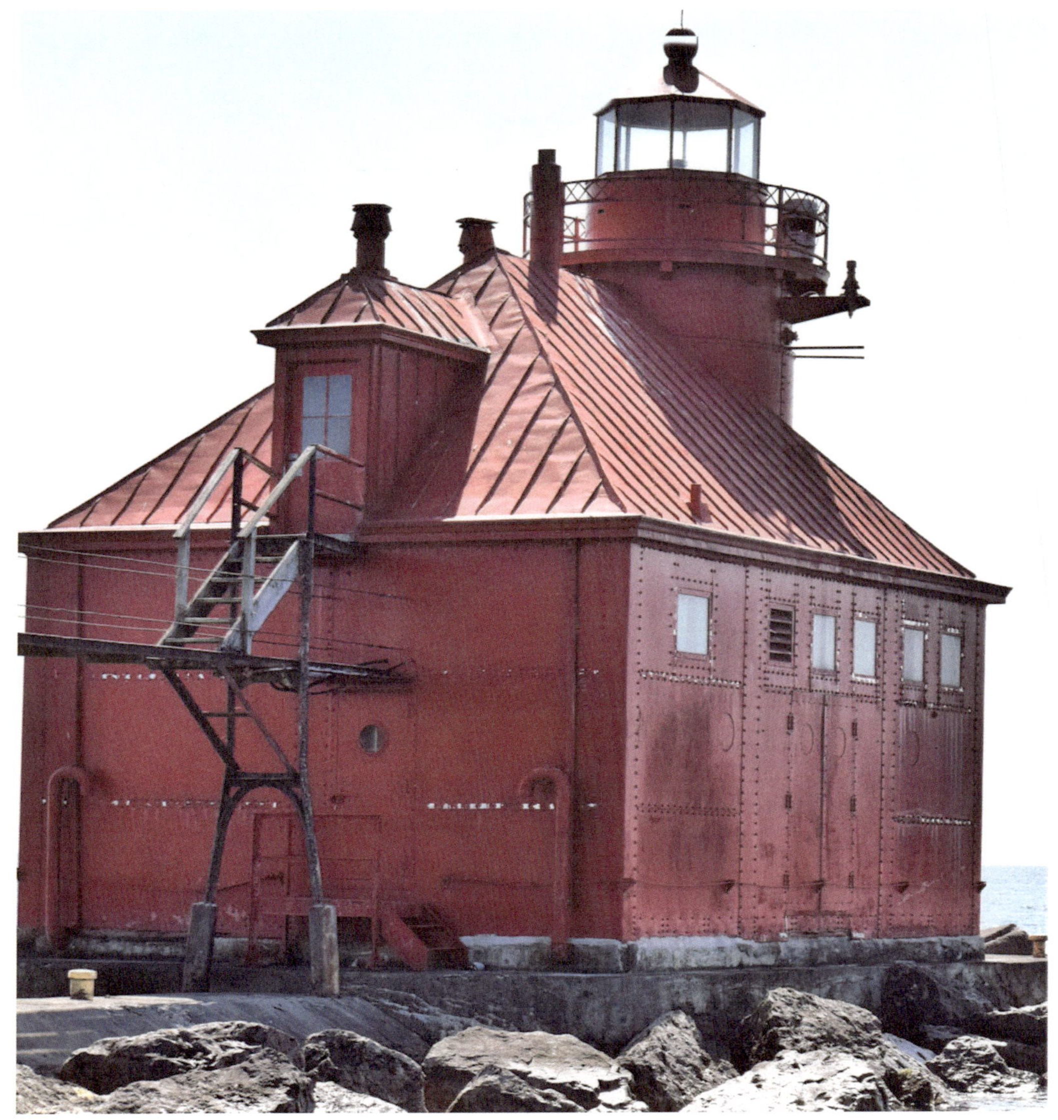

Construction of Current Structure: 1903 made of quarter-inch steel plates

Kewaunee Pierhead Lighthouse - Kewaunee, WI

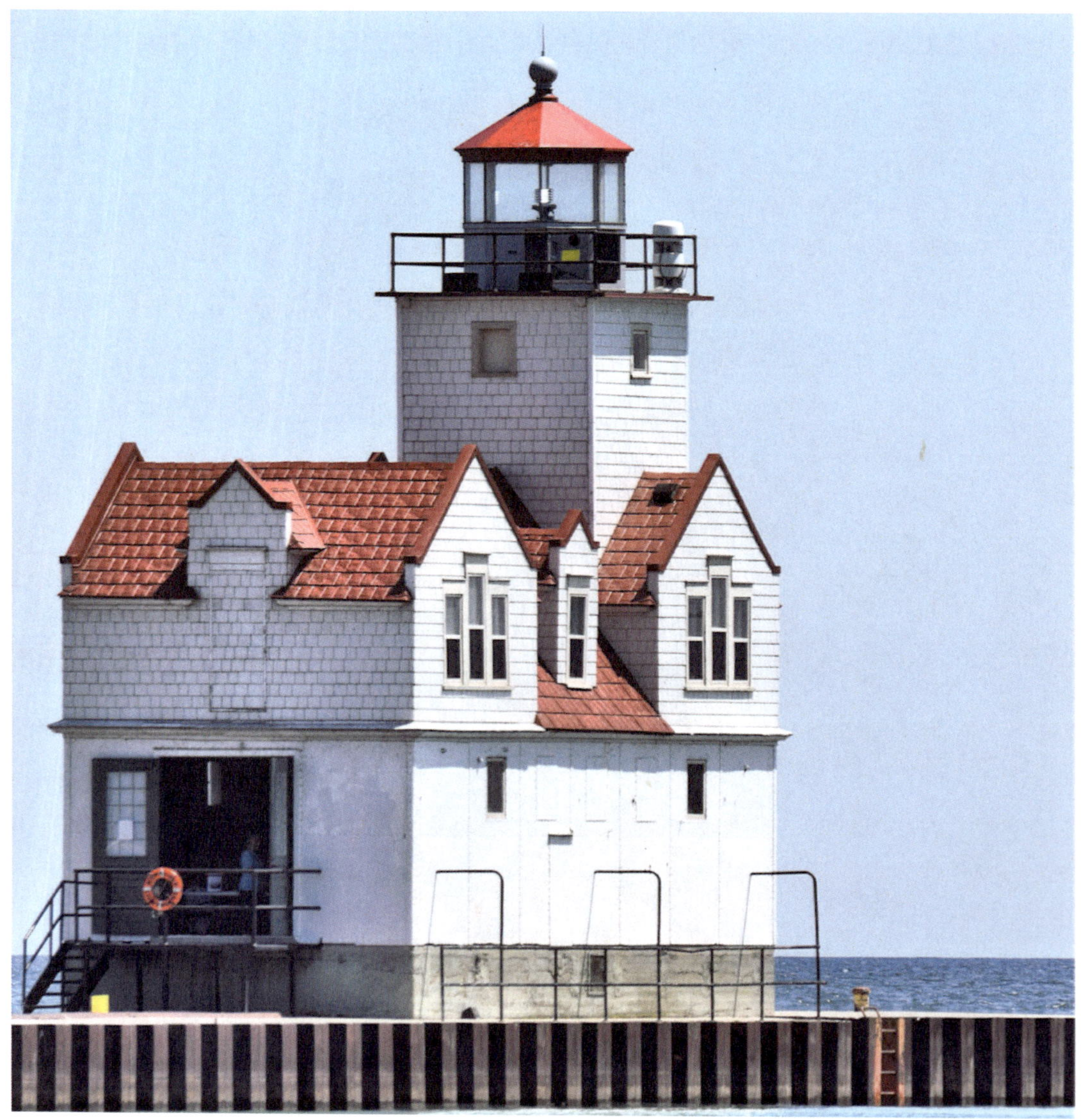

Constructed: 1912 - First Light Exhibited: 1913 - This structure identical to Holland, MI.

Port Washington Lighthouse - Port Washington, WI

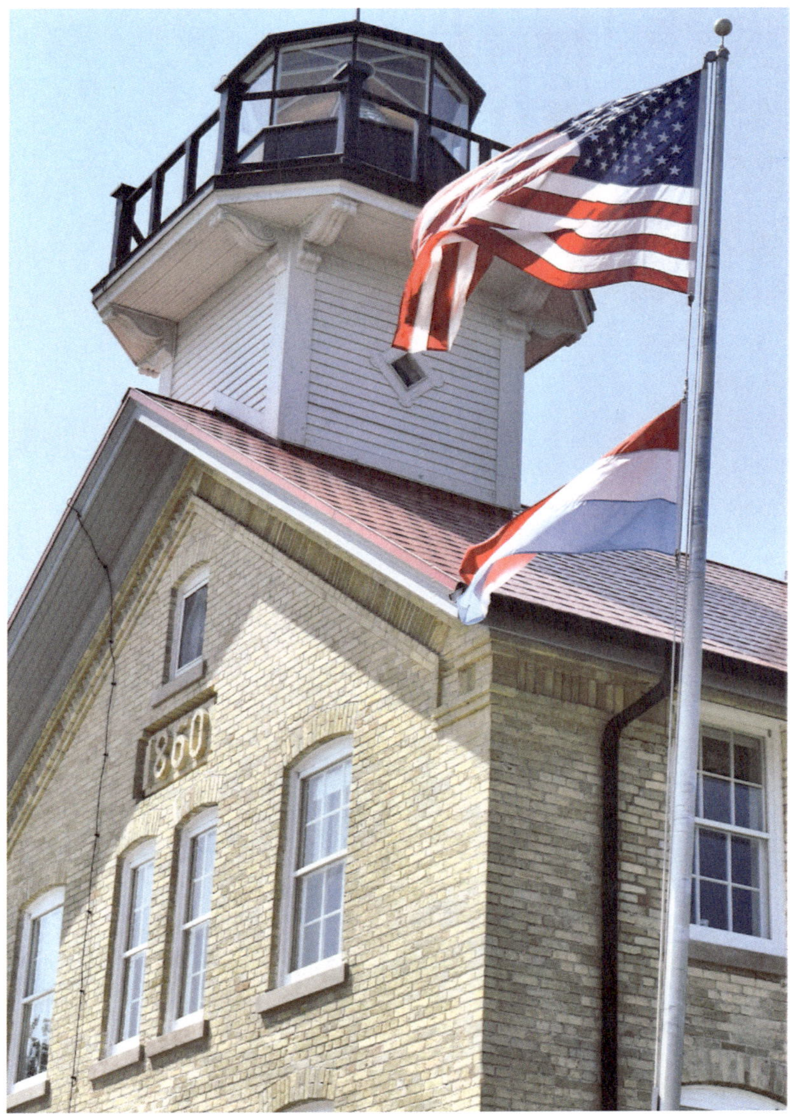

Constructed: Current structure 1860 - First Light Exhibited: 1849

Ownership: Port Washington Historical Society 1993 - National Register of Historic Places 1998

Rawley Point Lighthouse - Two Rivers, WI

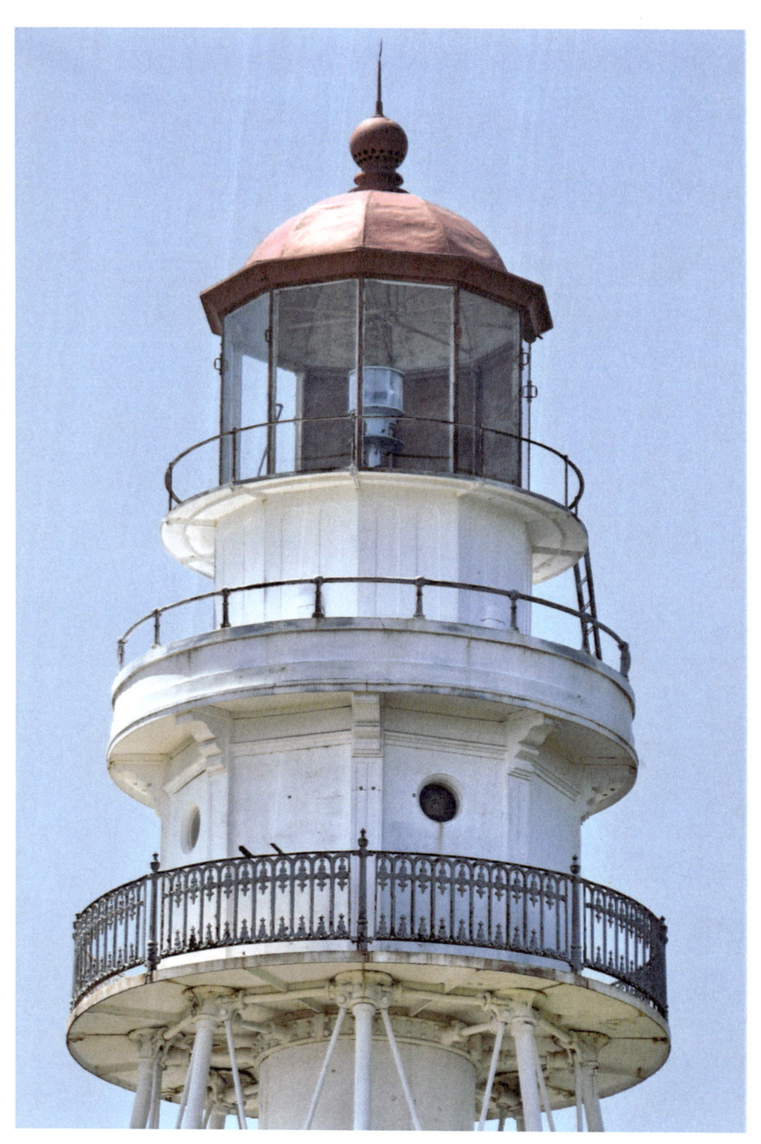

Main deck contains service room and watch room below the lantern gallery

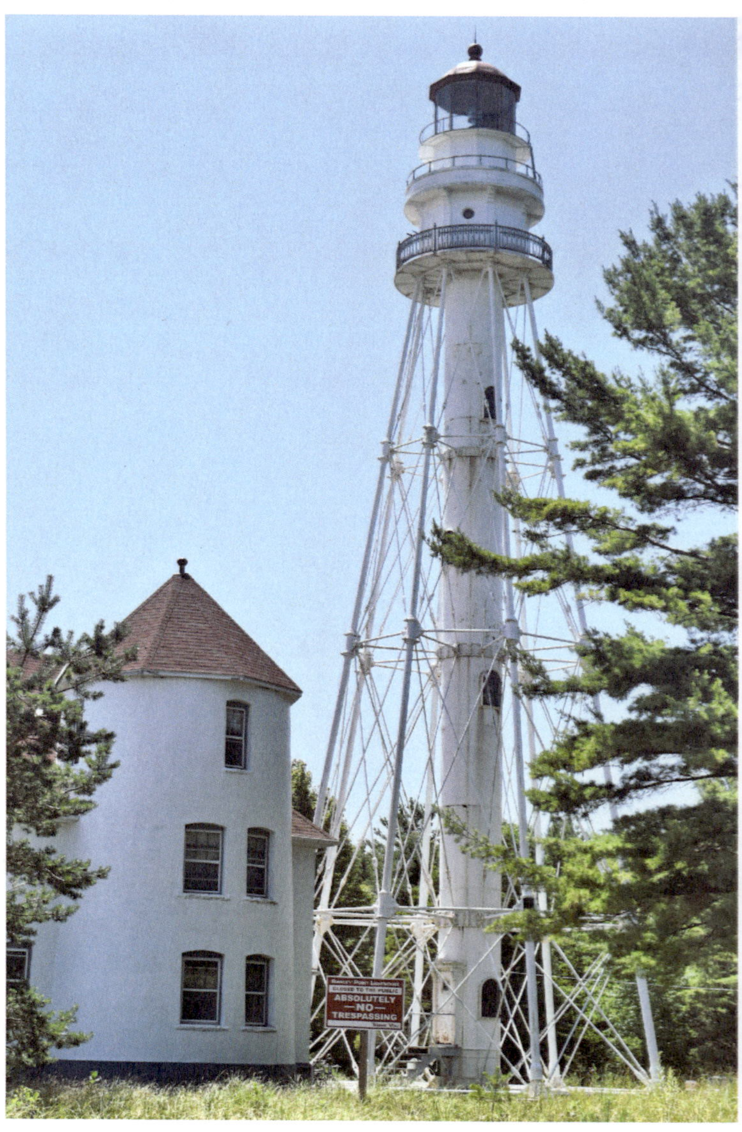

Tower Constructed: 1894 - Height: 113 feet
Tallest land-based lighthouse on the Great Lakes.

North Point Lighthouse - Milwaukee, WI

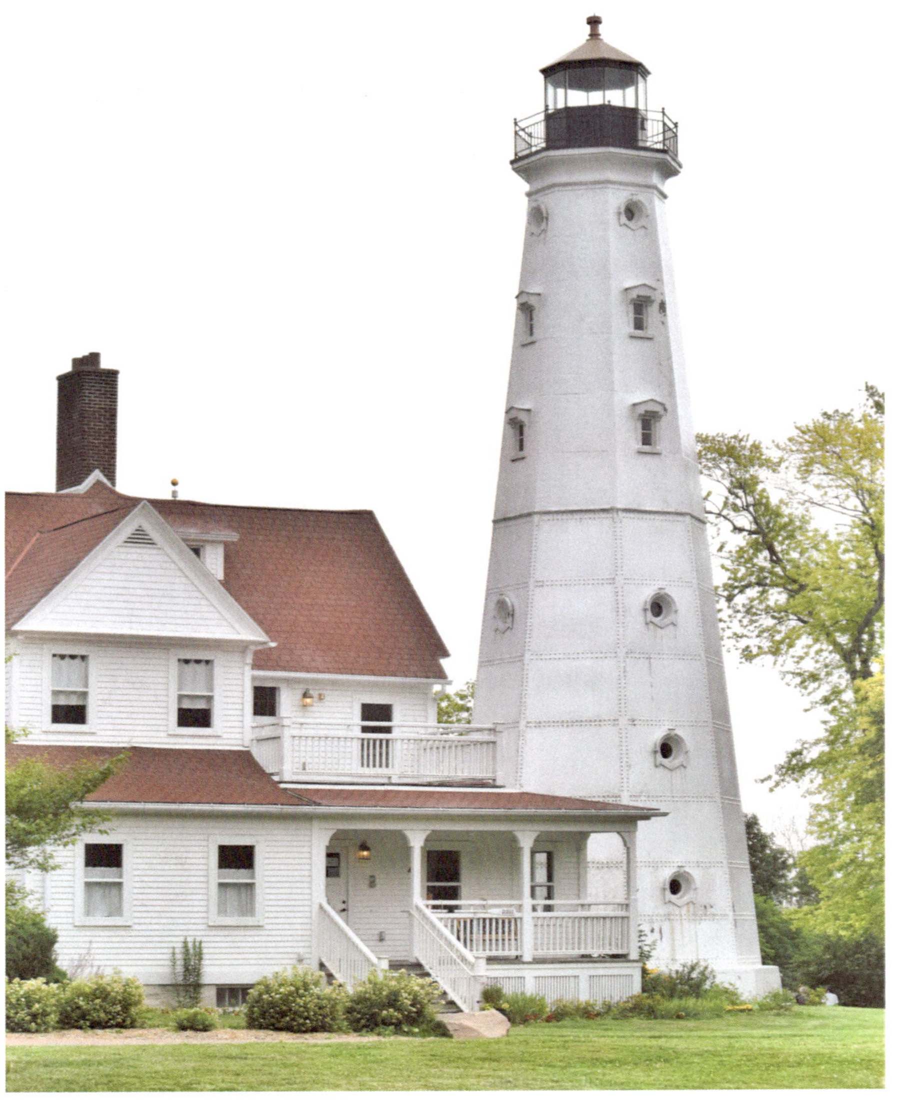

Constructed: Current Tower 1912 - First Light Exhibited: January 1888 - Height: 74 feet

National Register of Historical Place - Library of Congress Historic American Buildings Survey

Wind Point Lighthouse - Wind Point, WI

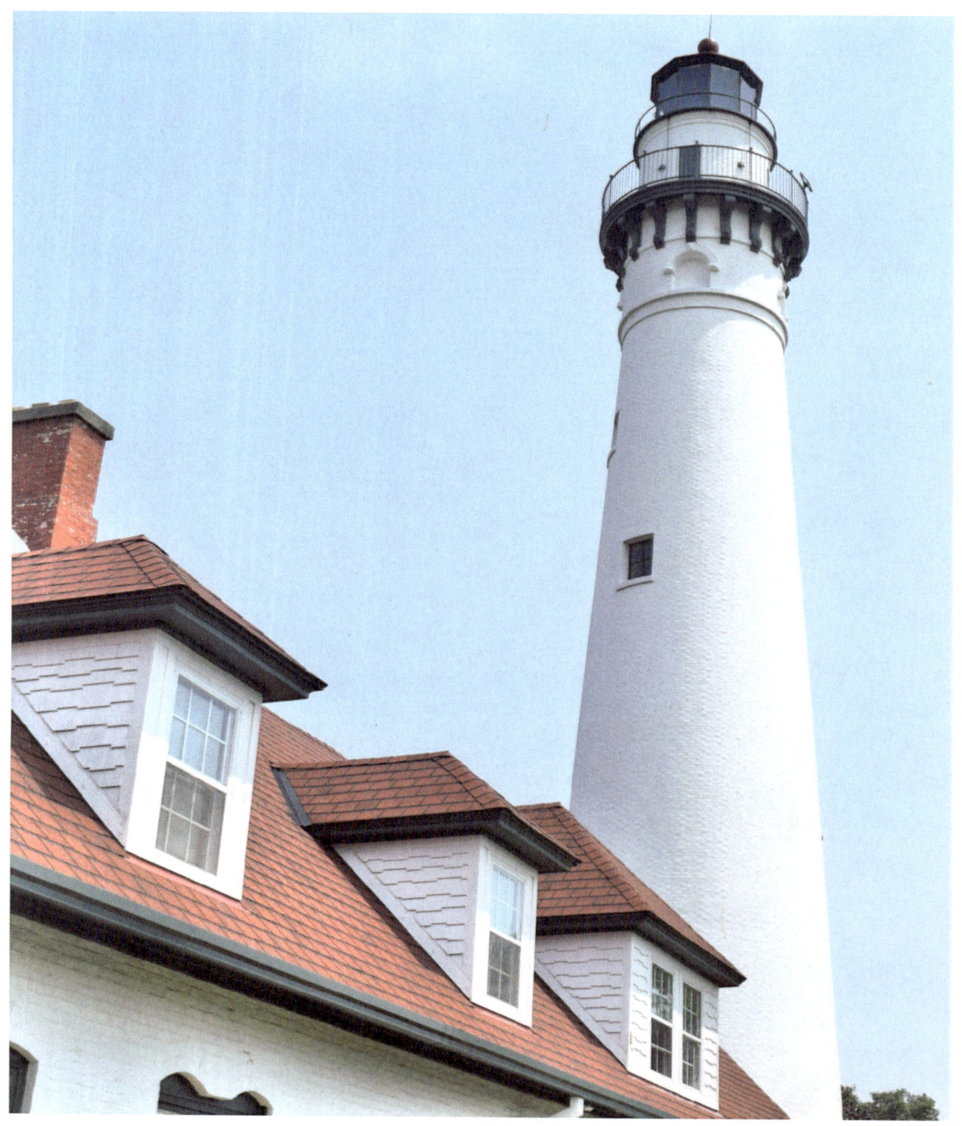

Constructed: 1879 - First Light Exhibited: November 1880 - Height 110 feet

Grosse Point Lighthouse - Evanston, IL

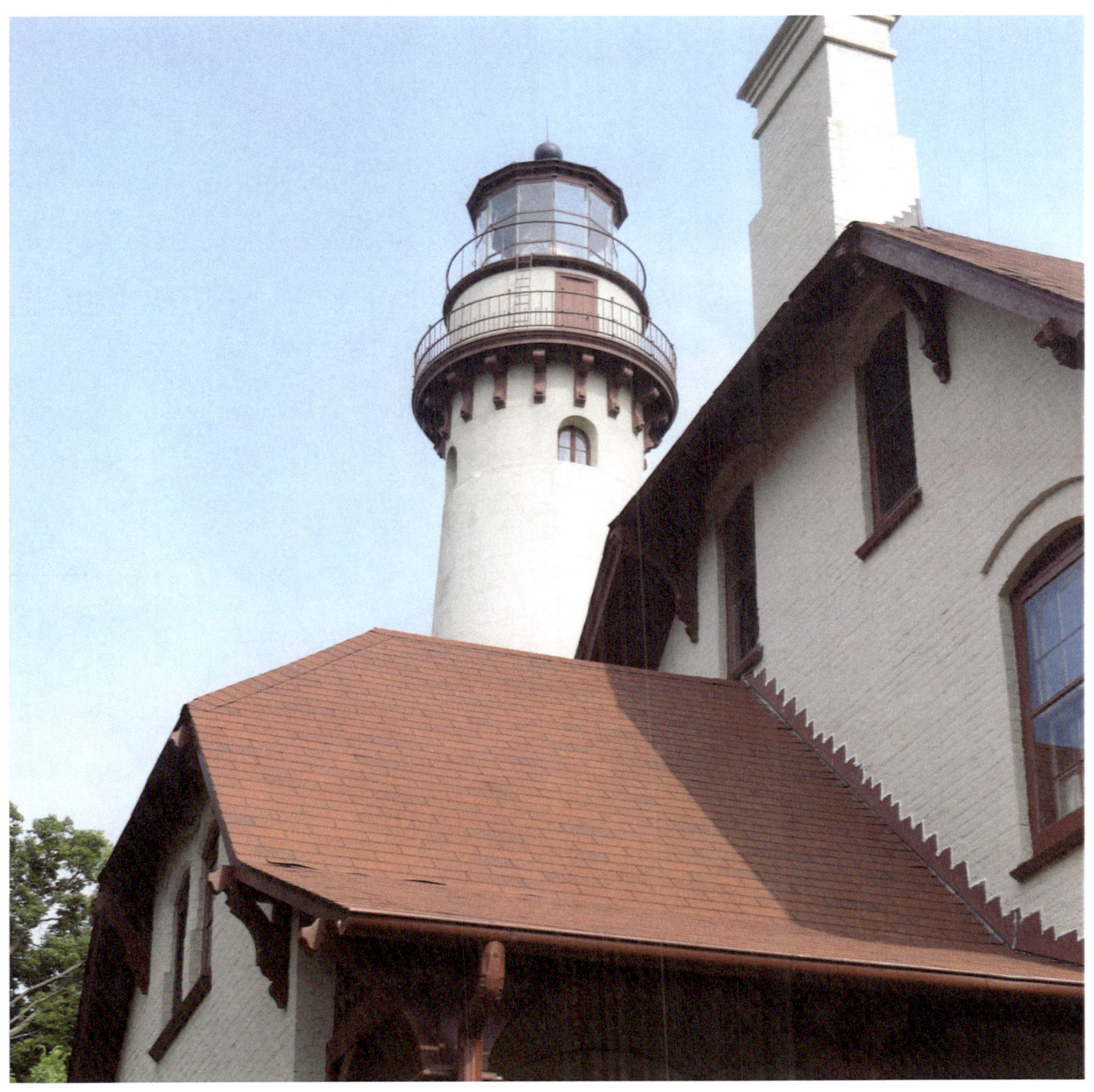

Constructed: 1873 - Light First Exhibited: March 1874 - Height: 113 feet

Old Michigan City Lighthouse
Michigan City, Indiana

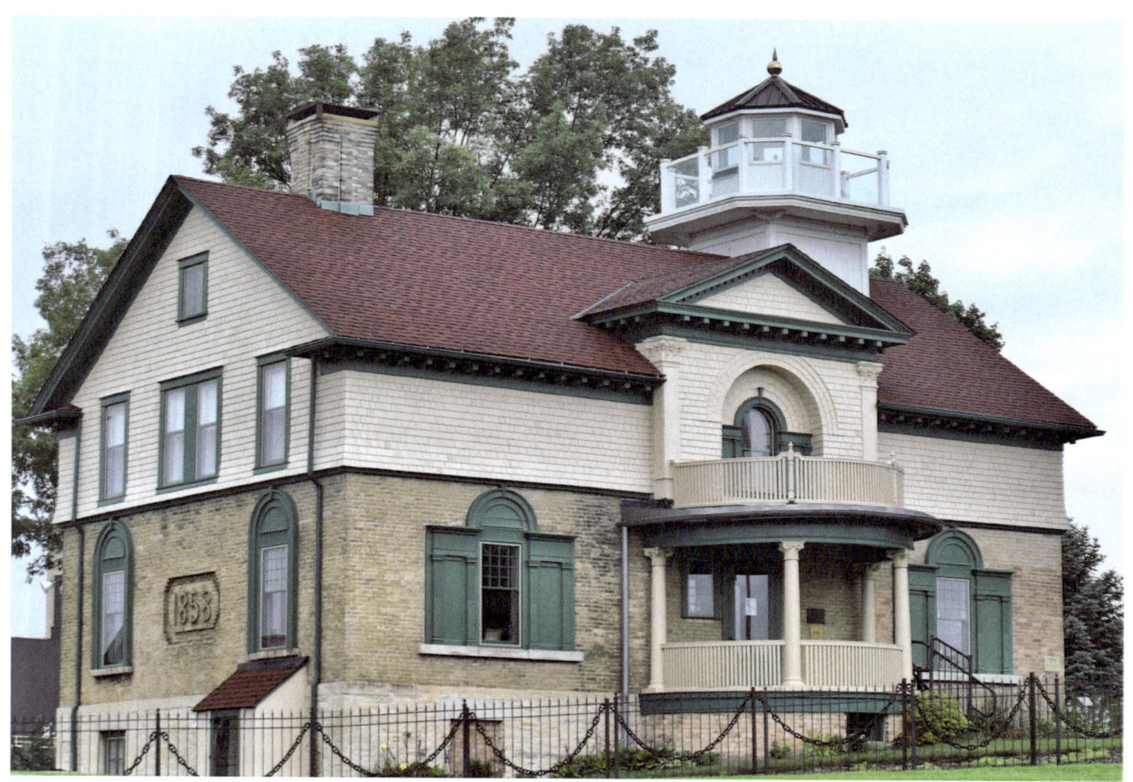

Constructed: 1858 - Light First Exhibited: Summer 1858
This is the second lighthouse for the community. Instead of constructing a separate tower and dwelling, a short, square, wooden tower was build atop the northern end of a new, seven-room dwelling. Renovated in 1963 by Michigan City Historical City, and 2003 by Hoosier Lighthousing Club.

Holland Harbor Lighthouse - Holland, MI

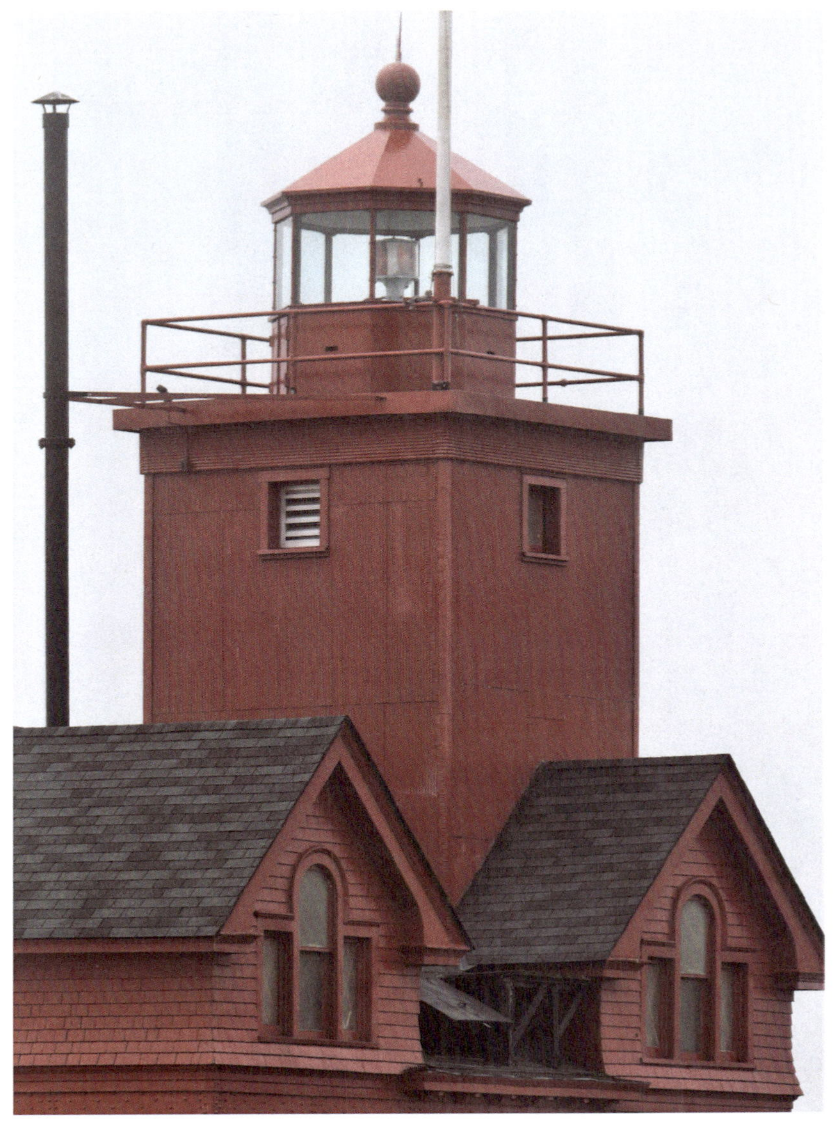

Constructed: 1936 - Light First Exhibited: 1907 - Painted red: 1956 - Locally known as Big Red

Design similar to the Kewaunee Pierhead Lighthouse in Kewaunee, WI

White River Lighthouse - White Lake, MI

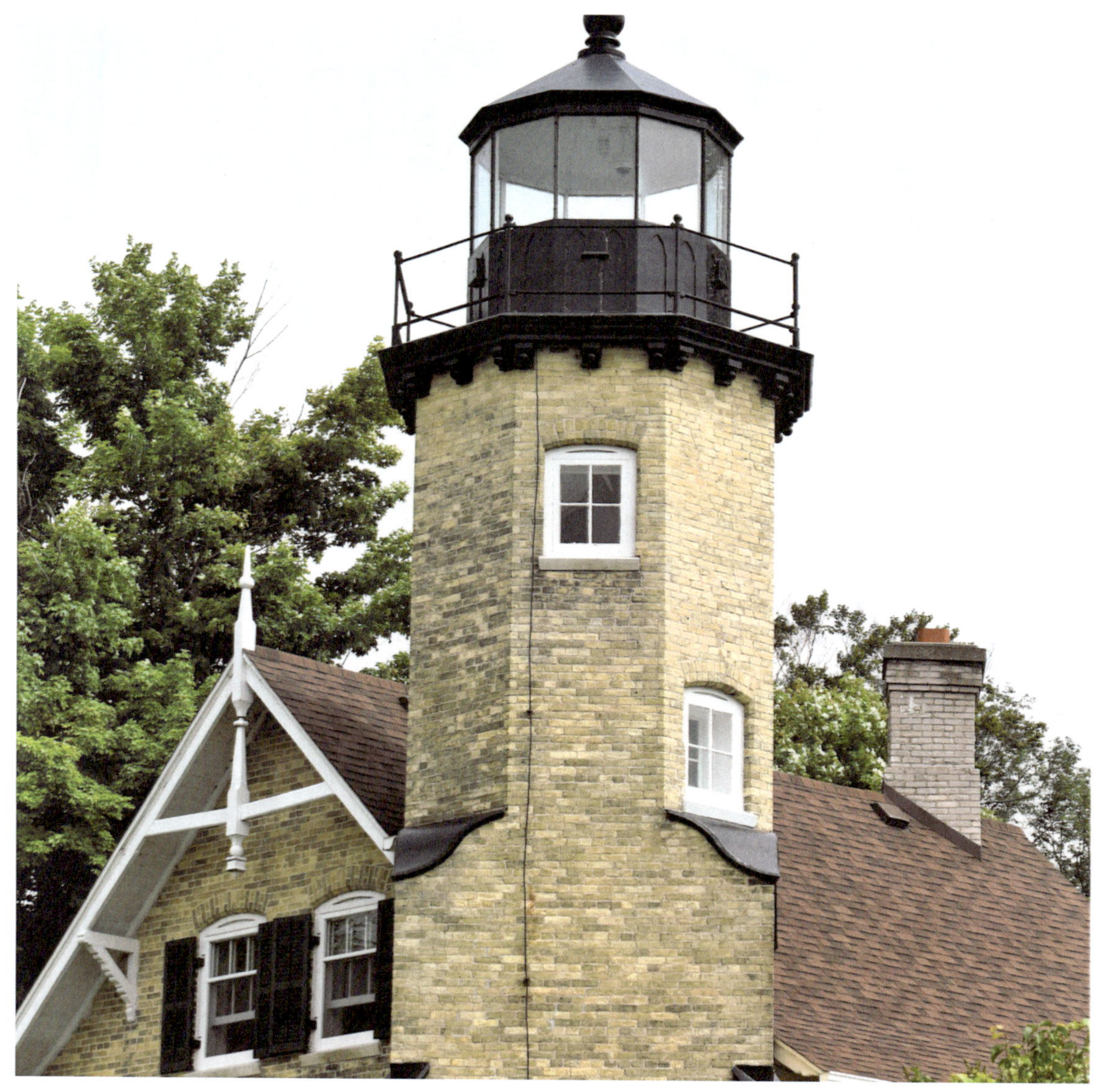

Construction: 1875 - Light First Exhibited: May 1876 - Norman Gothic design.

Little Sable Point Lighthouse - Silver Lake State Park, MI

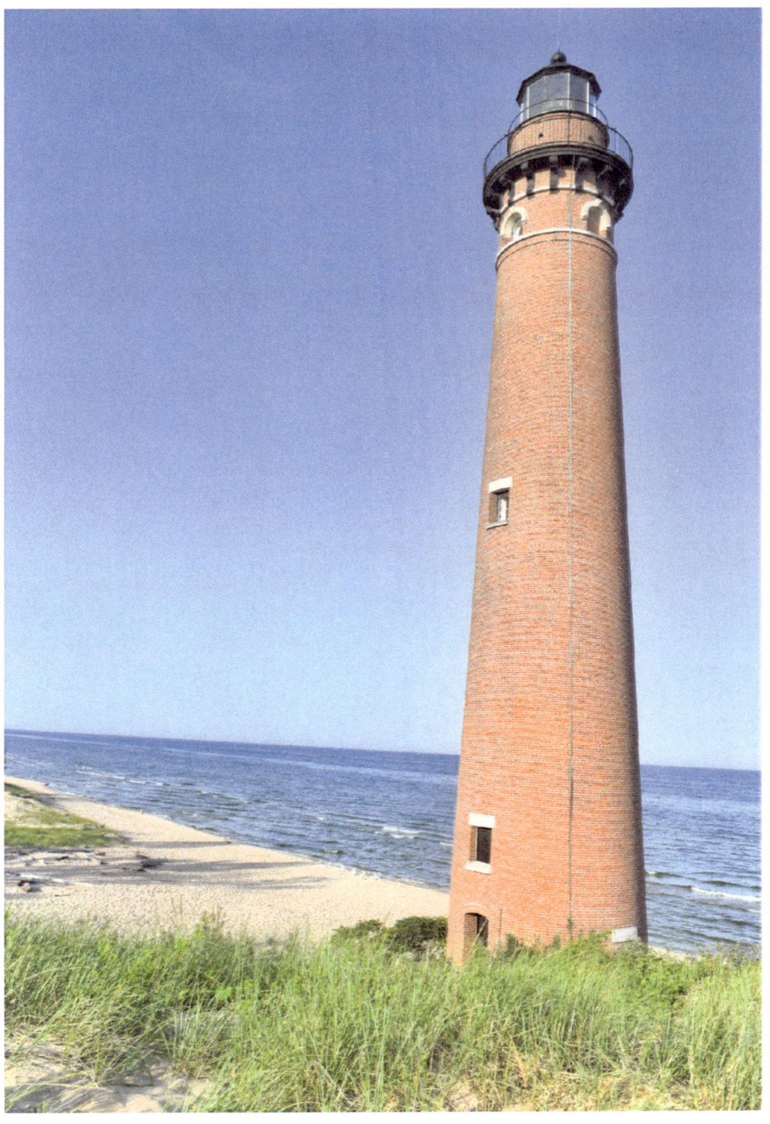

Constructed: 1873 - Light First Exhibited: 1874 - Height: 100 feet

Point Betsie Lighthouse - Frankfort, MI

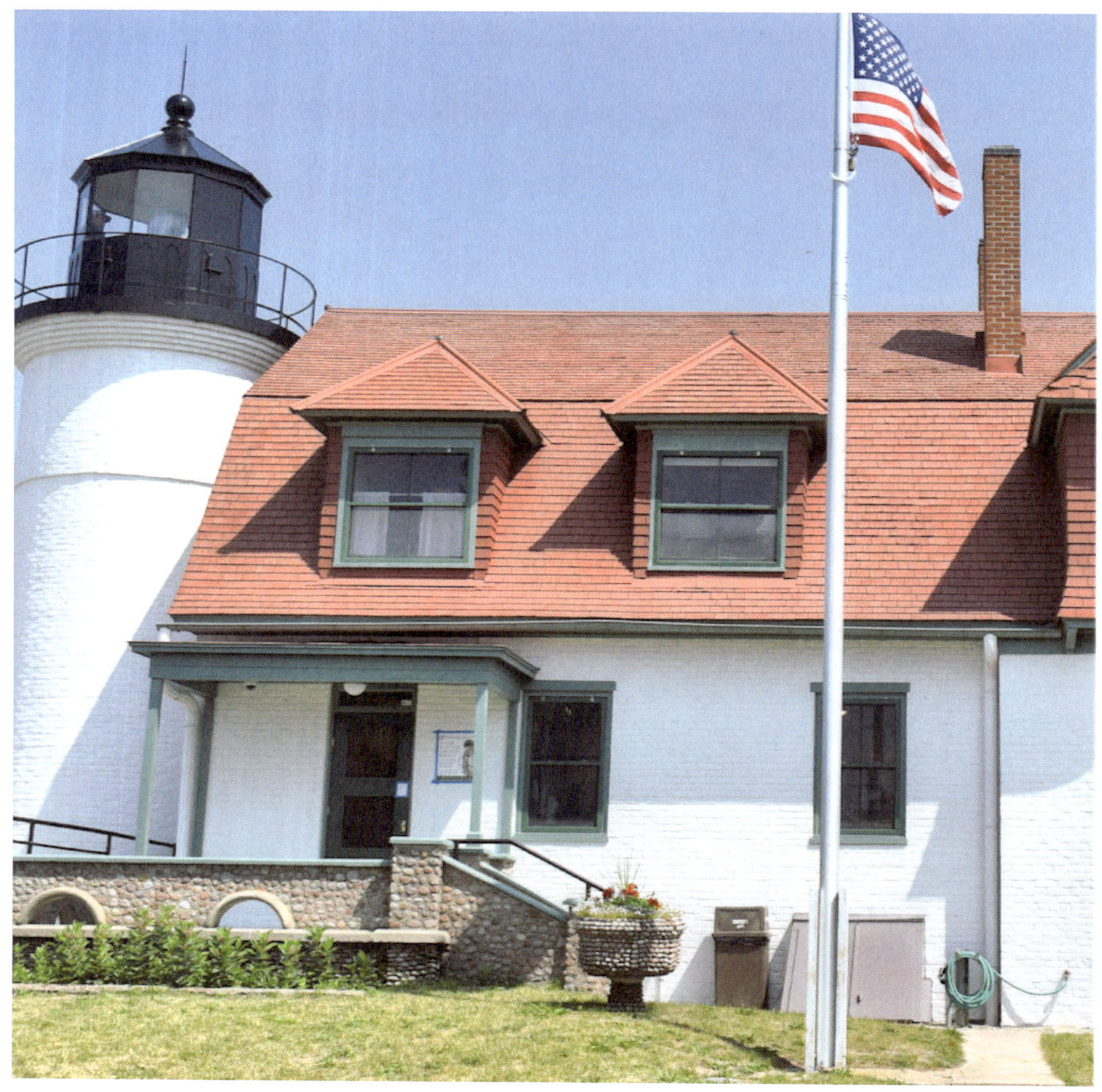

Construction: 1854 - First Light Exhibited: October 1858 - Height: 39 feet
Life saving station established: 1875.
Owned by Benzie County 2004 - National Register of Historical Places
Point Besie is one of America's most photograhed lighthouses.

Grand Traverse Lighthouse - Grand Traverse Bay, Michigan

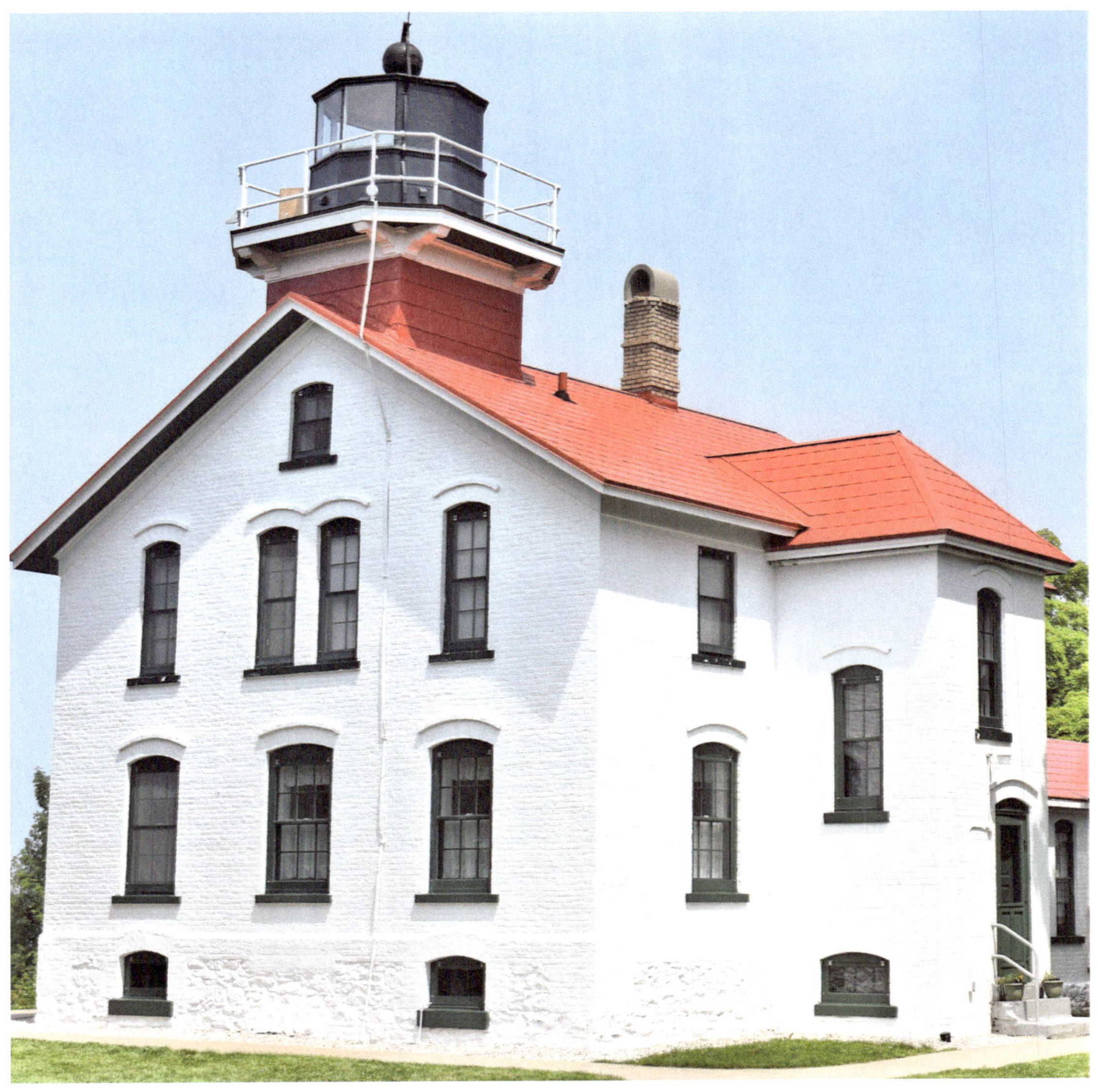

Constructed: 1858 - Light First Exhibited: 1858

Mission Point Lighthouse - Grand Traverse Bay, Michigan

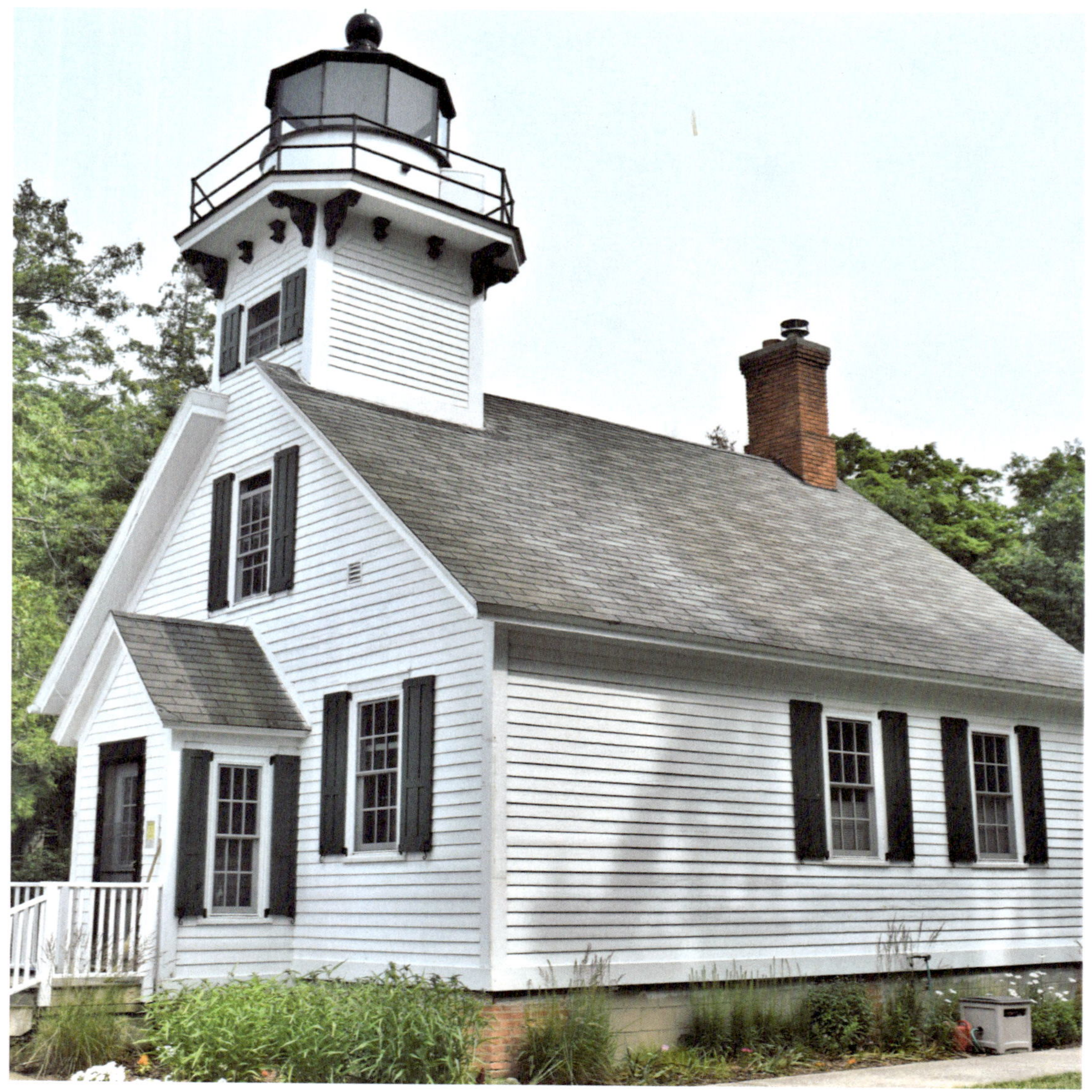

Constructed: 1870 - Light First Exhibited: September 1870 - Height: 35 feet

McGulpin's Point Lighthouse - Mackinaw City, MI

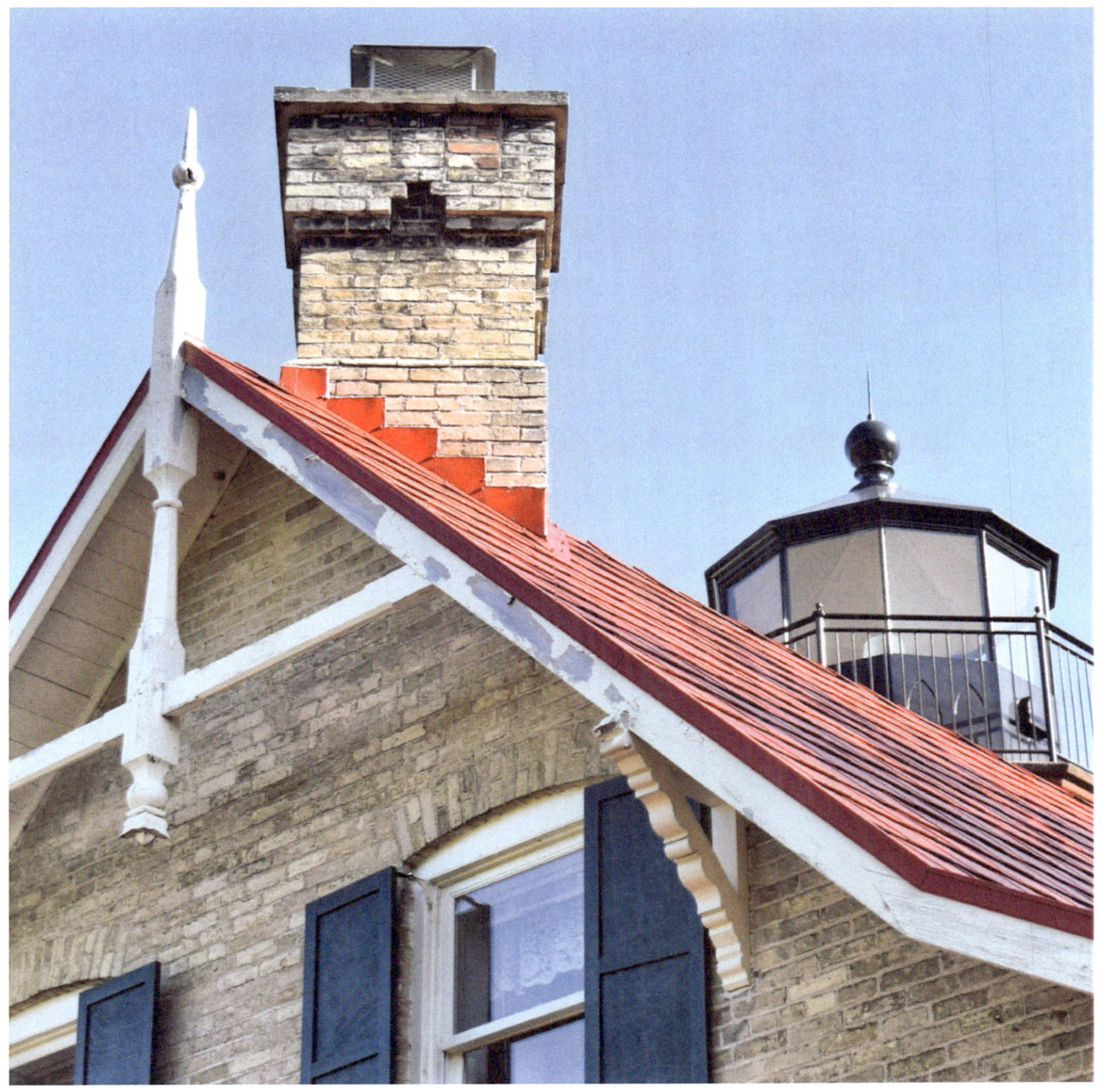

Constructed: 1868 - Light First Exhibited: June 1869 - Height: 40 feet - Norman Gothic stype

Lake Huron

Mackinaw Bridge, which connects the 'mitten' of Michigan to the Upper Peninsula, is where Lake Michigan and Lake Huron meet. Our journey follows the east side of Michigan to Detroit. Along the way I learned about range lighthouses, crib light, lightships and climbed to several of the towers' lantern rooms.

Aligning two fixed lights on land provides a navigator with a line of position called a range. When the two lights align vertically the ship is on the correct course.

Crib lights are towers without a dwelling, frequently located on breakwater piers. Crib refers to the wooden pier style of construction which was used as a foundation for the light tower.

Lightship Huron, anchored in Huron City north of Detroit, is a ship that acts as a lighthouse. These ships are used in waters that are too deep or otherwise unsuitable for lighthouse construction.

Many of the lighthouses were open for tours, including climbing to the lantern room. The tallest, and therefore, the most steps, was Presque Isle New Lighthouse with 130 steps. In the captions about each lighthouse I have given you the height of the tower so you can appreciate lightkeeper's climbing to the lantern room to fill the lamp with oil, sometime three times during a night.

Lake Huron is connected to Lake Erie by St. Clair River, St. Clair Lake and the Detroit River. There were no lighthouses with dwellings along this route.

Old Mackinac Point Lighthouse - Mackinaw City, MI

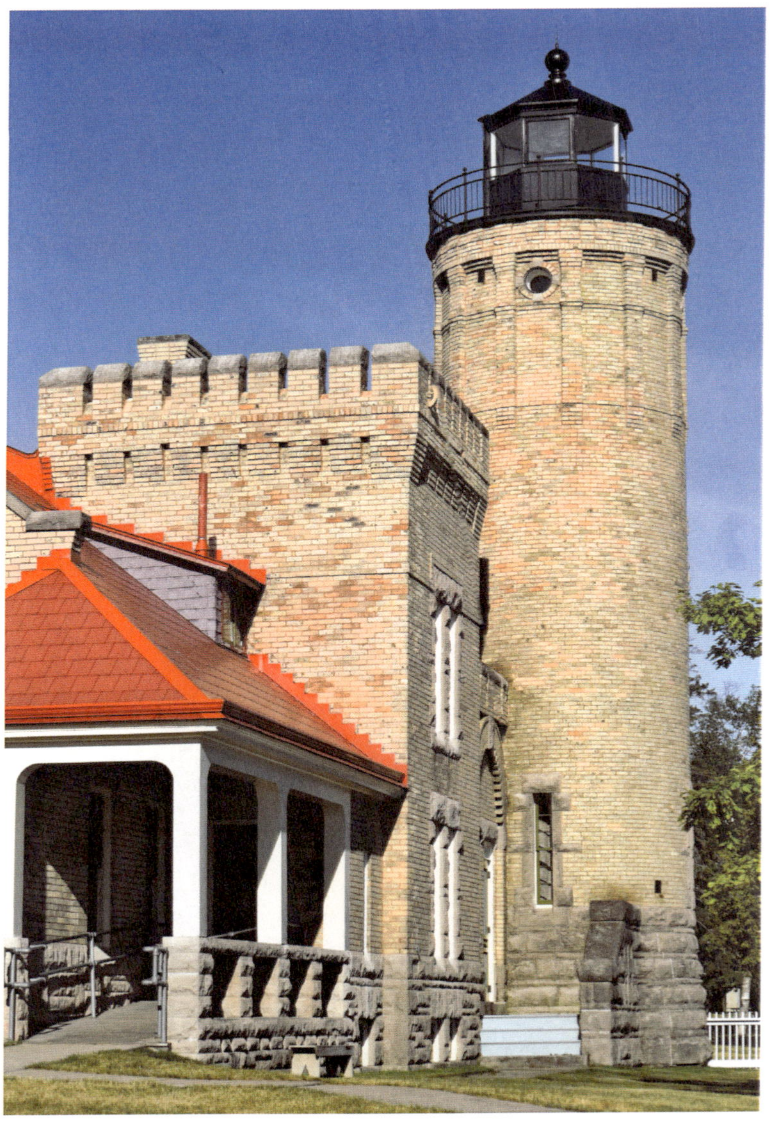

Constructed: 1892 - Light First Exhibited: October 1892 - Height: 45 feet

Located in the Michilimackinac State Historic Park adjacent to the Mackinac Bridge.

Cheboygan Crib Lighthouse - Cheboygan, MI

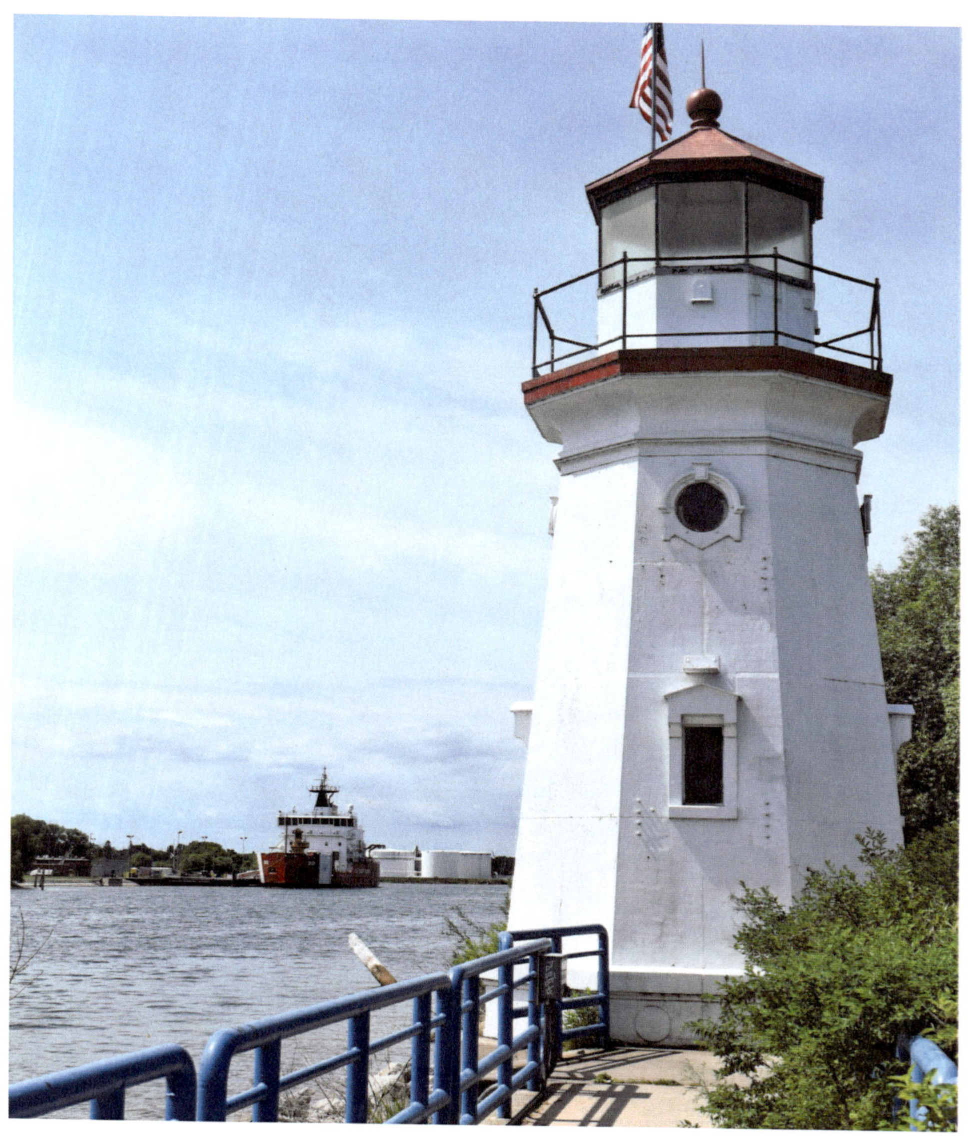

Constructed: 1884 - Light First Exhibited: November 1884 - Height: 33 feet
The lighthouse was original on a man-made island marking the mouth of the Cheboygan River.

Forty Mile Point Lighthouse - Hammond Bay, Michigan

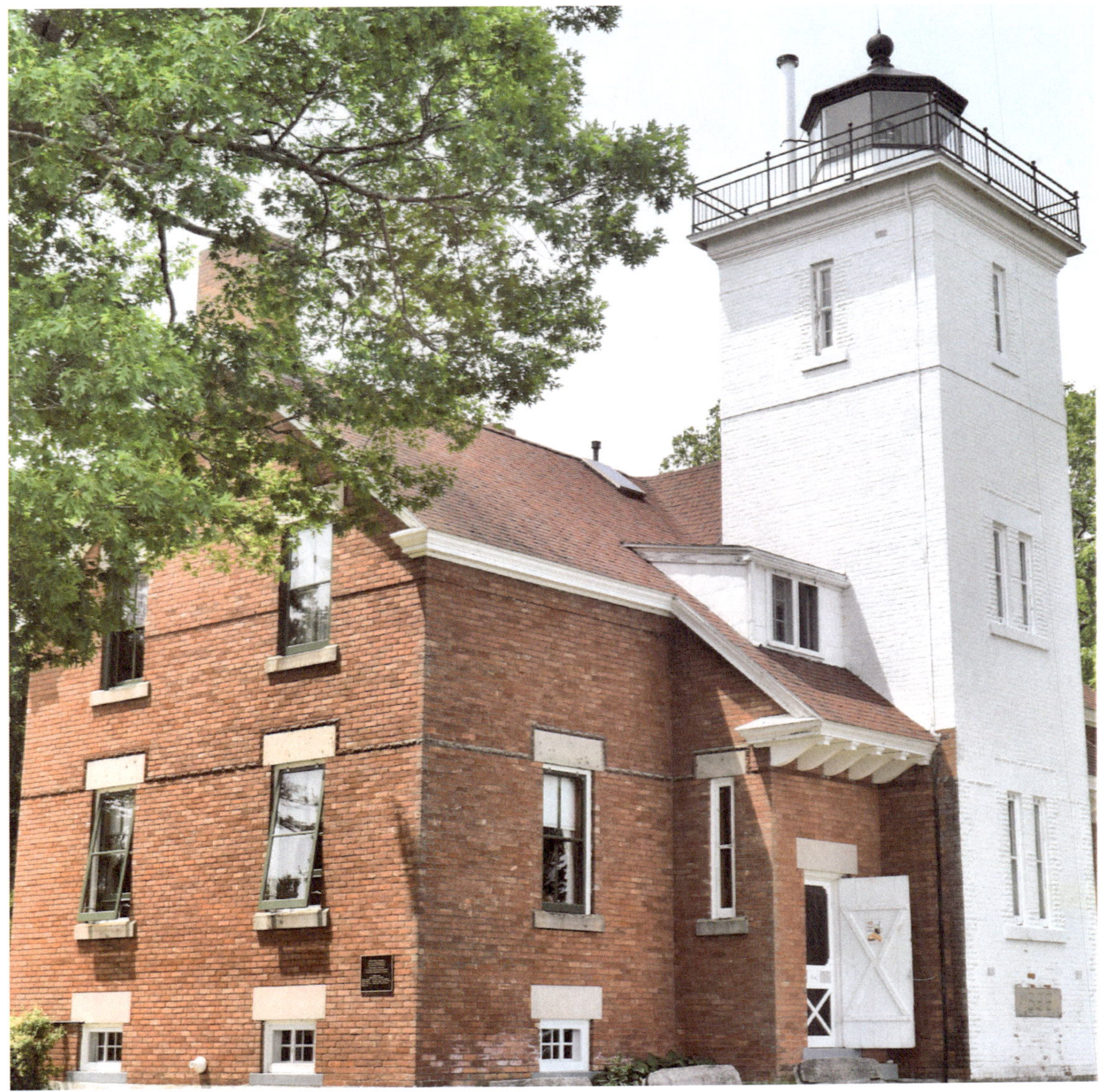

Constructed: 1896 - Light First Exhibited: April 1897 - Height: 52 feet

Old Presque Isle Lighthouse - Presque Isle Harbor, Michigan

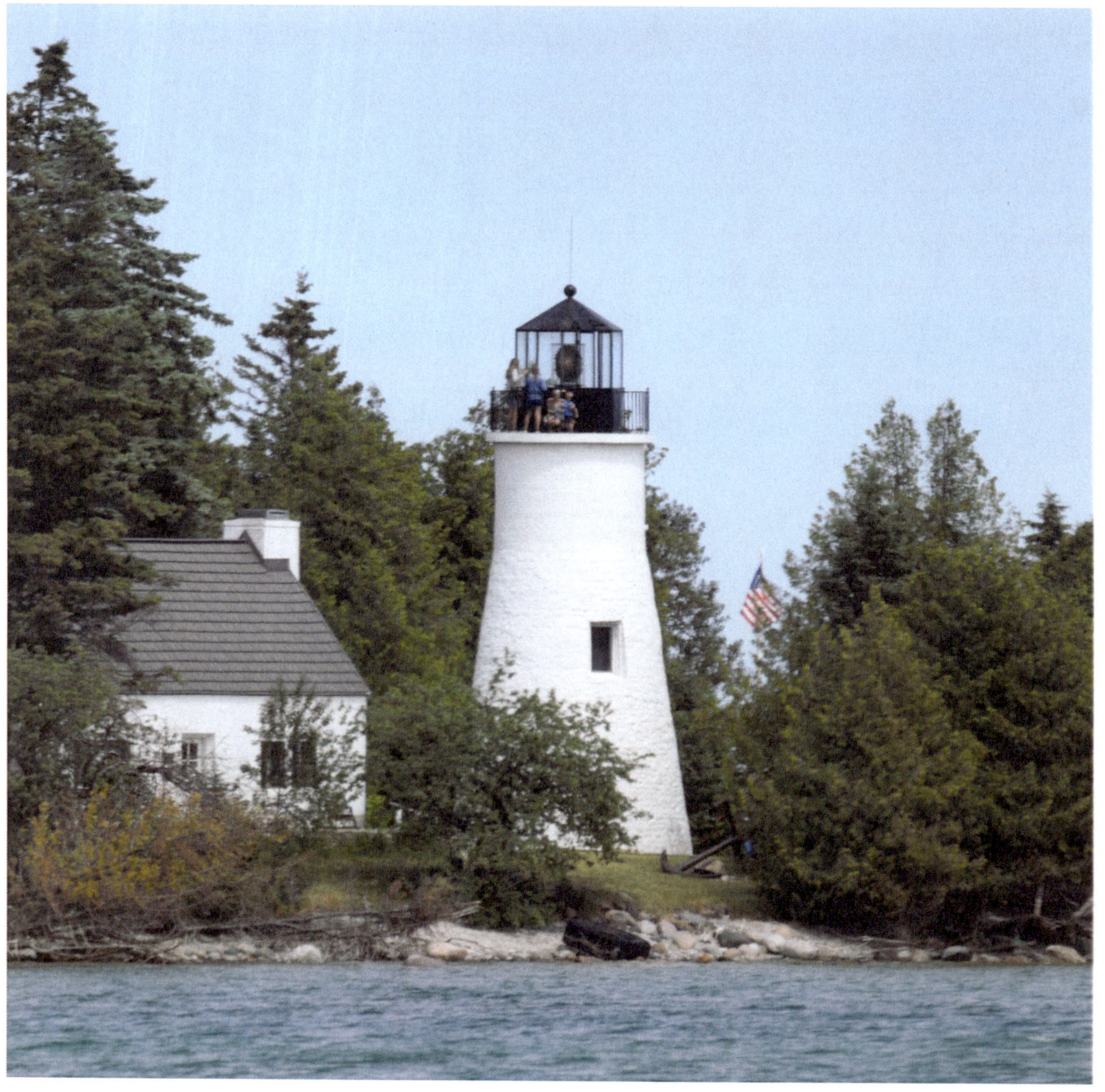

Constructed: 1840 - Light First Exhibited: August 1840 - Height: 31 feet

Presque Isle New Lighthouse - Presque Isle Harbor, MI

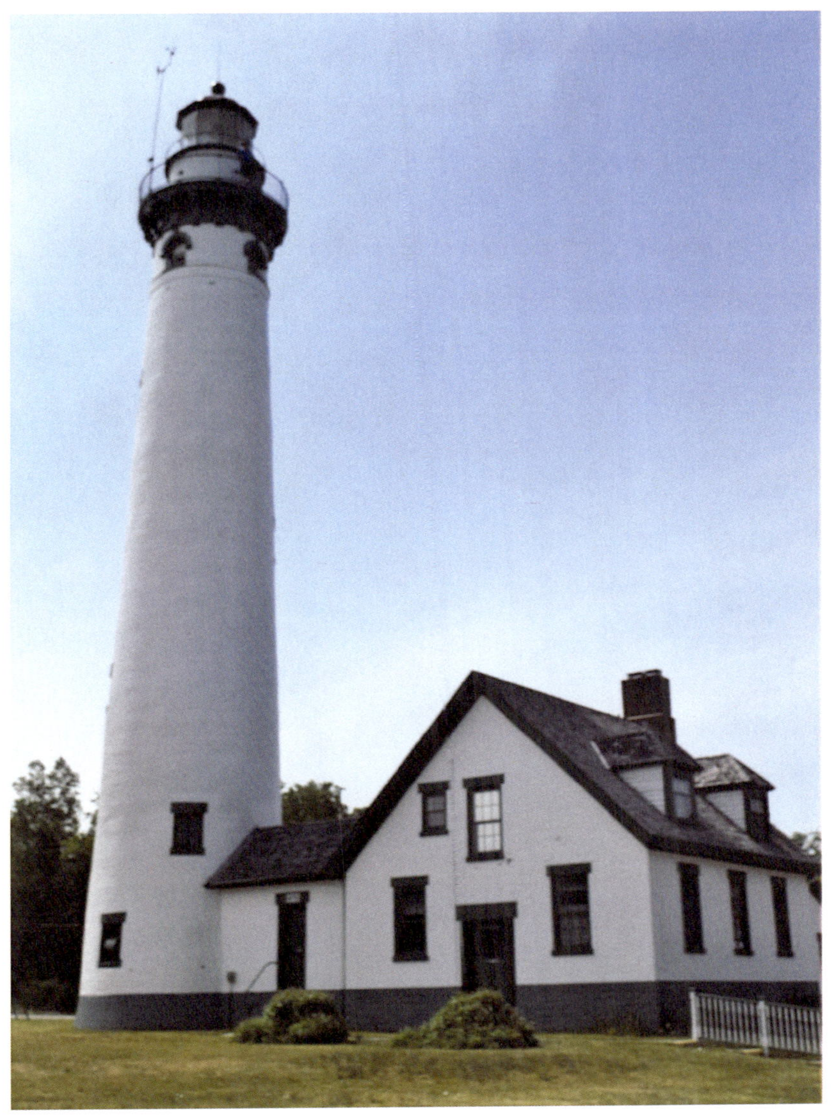

Constructed: 1870 - Light First Exhibited: Spring 1871 - Height: 113.5 feet (130 steps to top)

Sturgeon Point Lighthouse - Saginaw Bay, MI

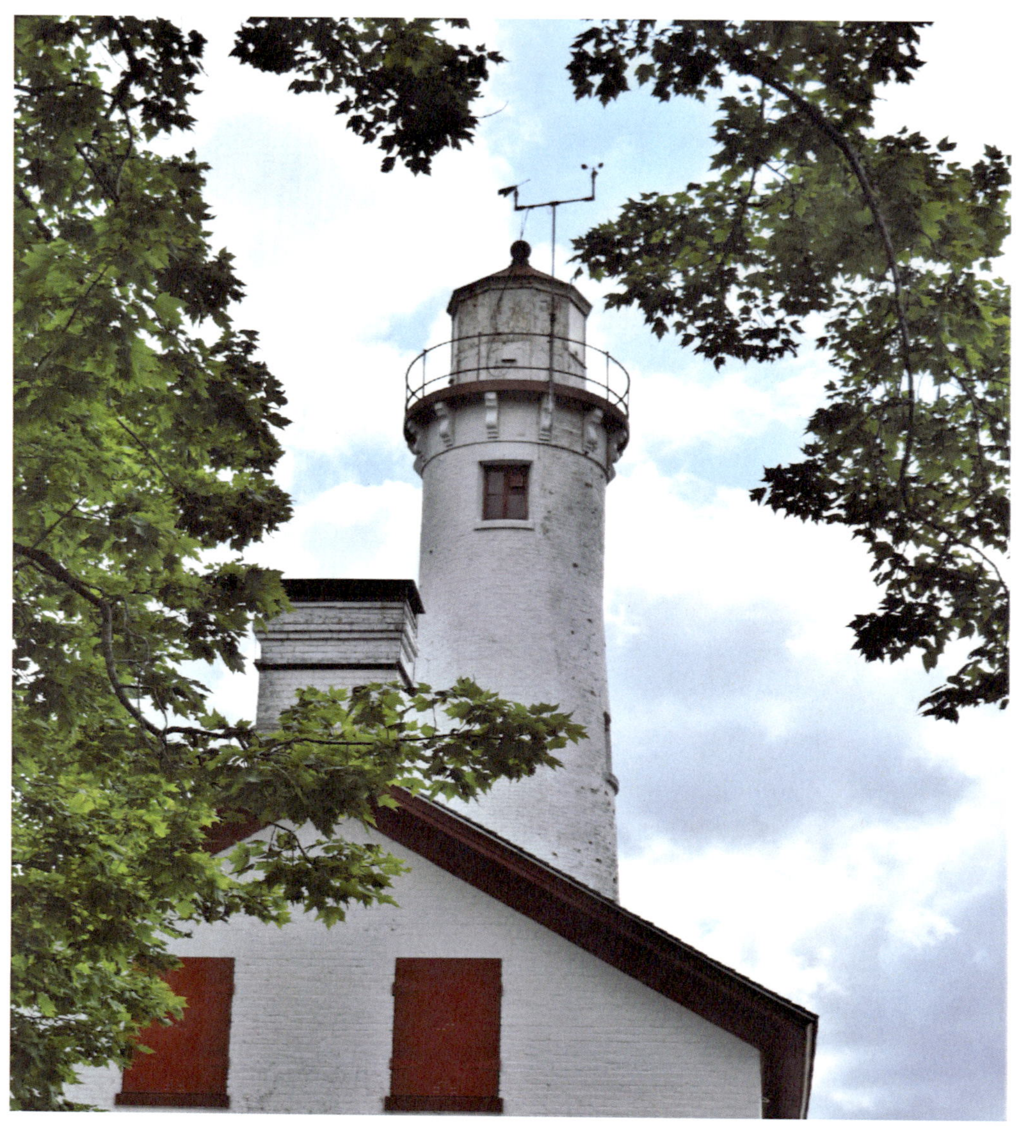

Constructed: 1870 - Light First Exhibited: Spring 1871 - Height: 70 feet 9 inches

Tawas Point Lighthouse - Tawas City, MI

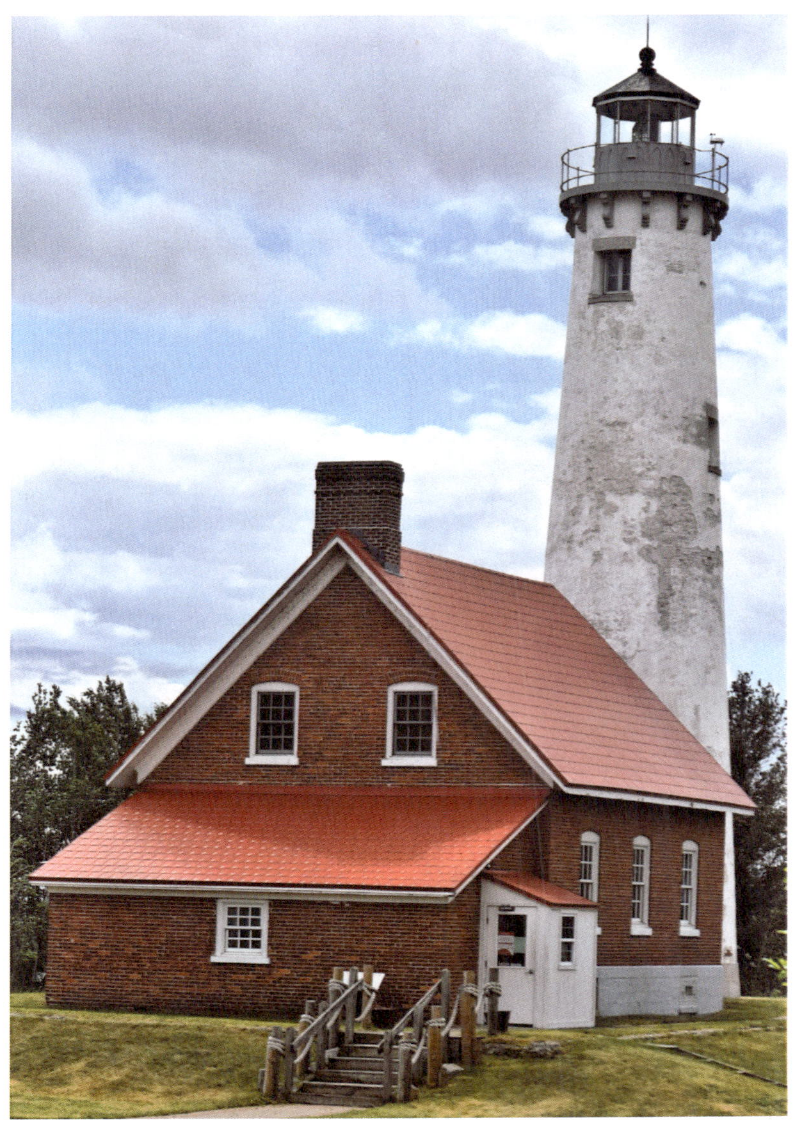

Constructed: 1876 - Light First Exhibited: Spring 1877 - Height: 67 feet 3 inches

Pointe aux Barques Lighthouse - Michigan

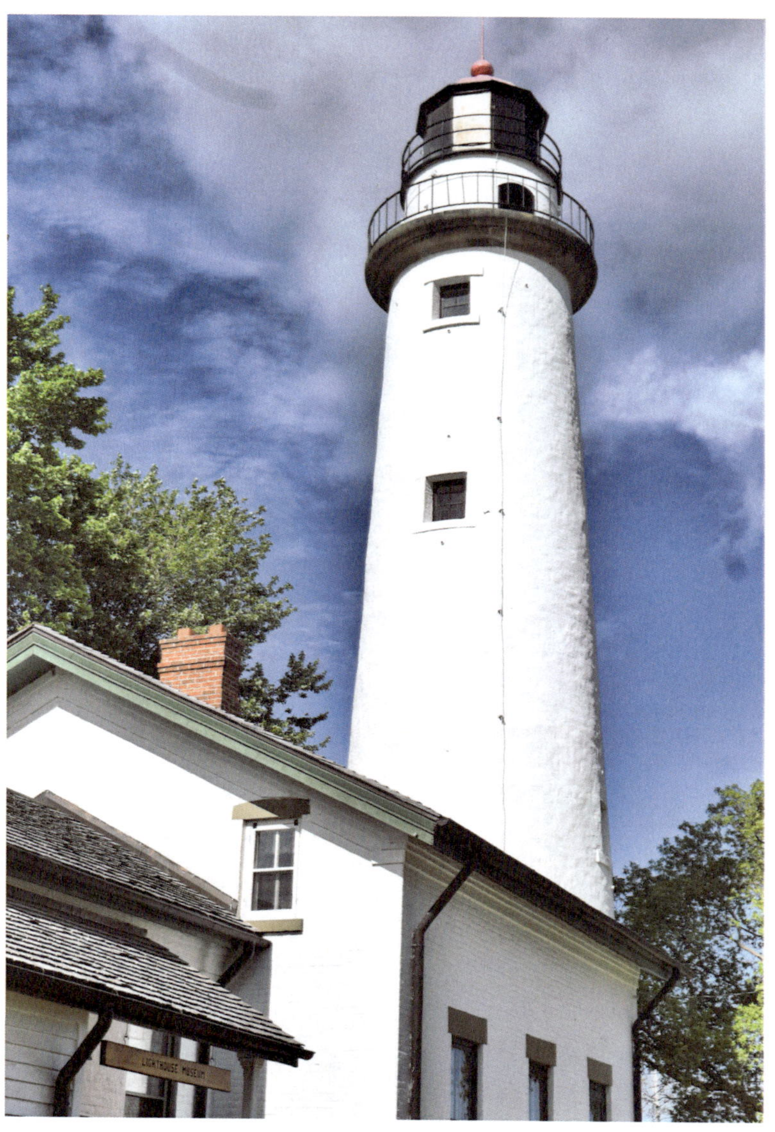

Constructed: 1857 - Light First Exhibited: Spring 1858 - Height 79 feet

Fort Gratiot Lighthouse - Port Huron, MI

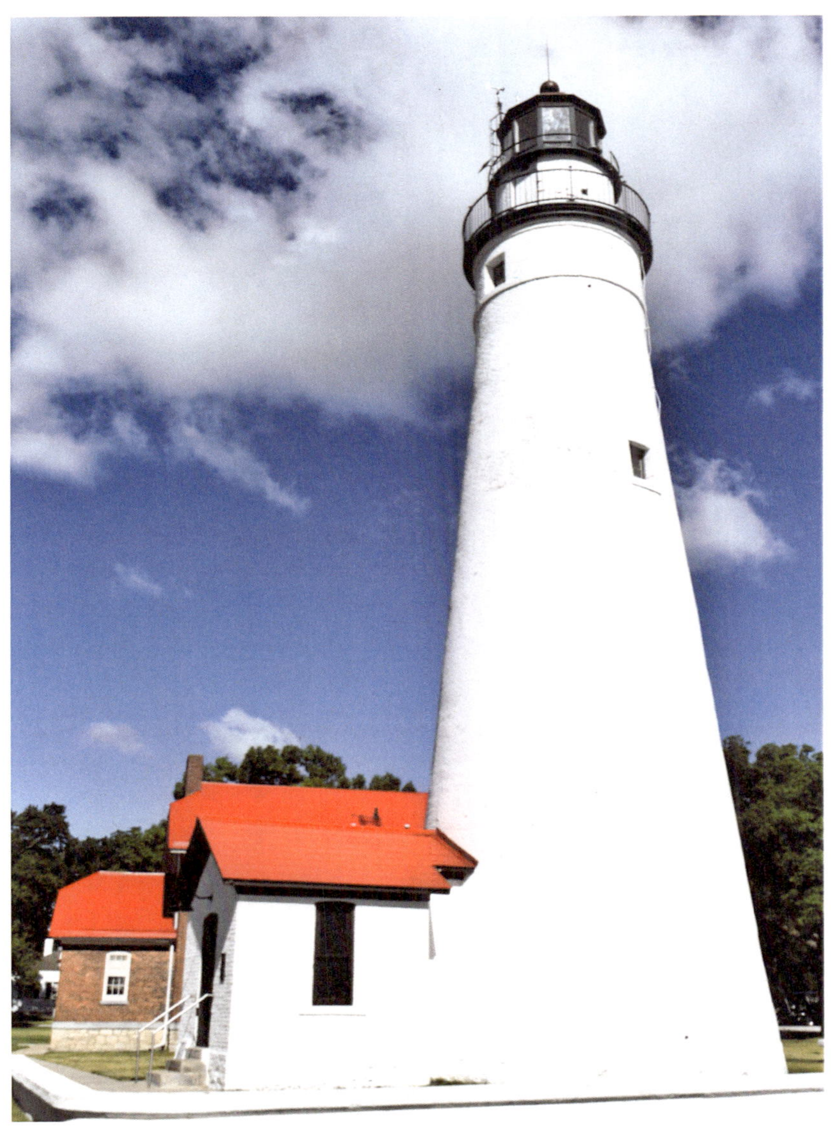

Constructed: 1829 - Light First Exhibited: 1829 - Height: 89 feet

Lightship Huron - Port Huron, MI

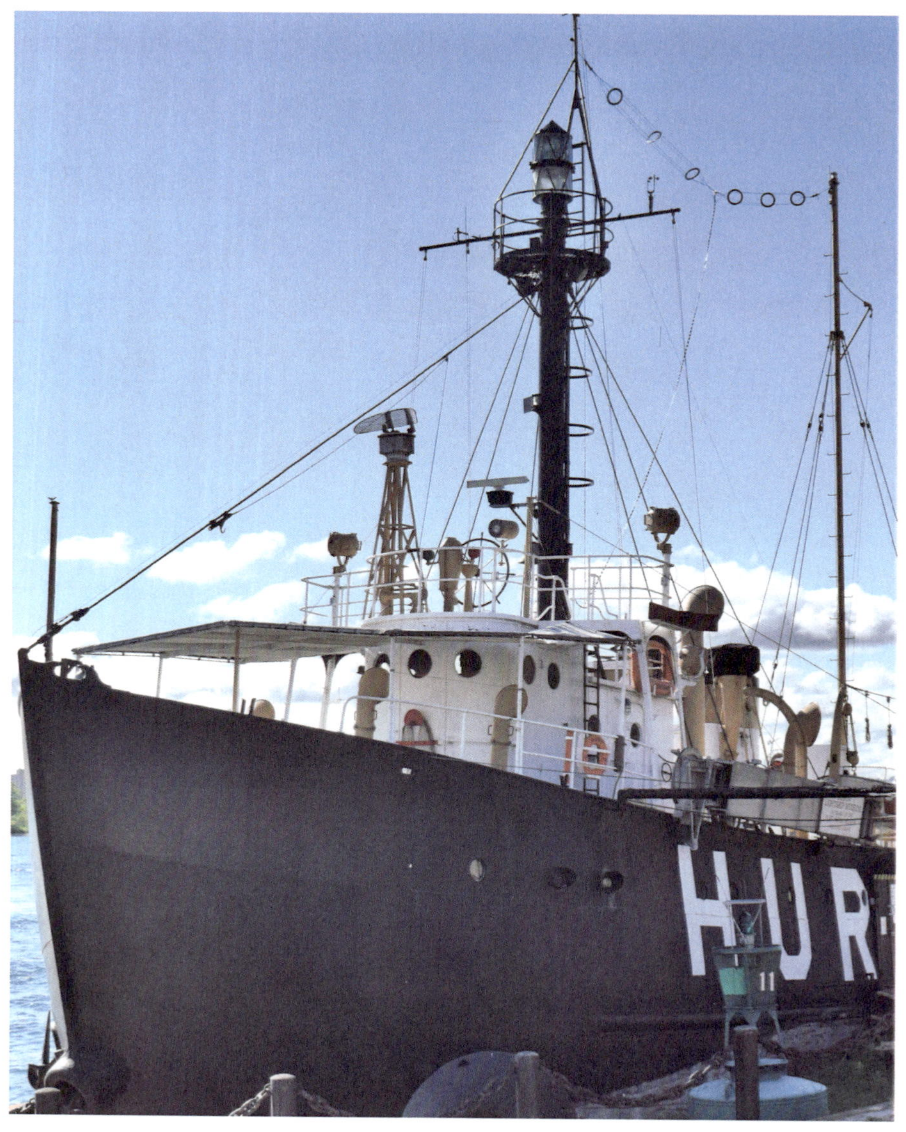

Served: 1893-1920 - It sailed along the Corsica Shoals, Grays Reef, and North Manitou Shoal -
90 feet long

Peche Island Lighthouse - Marine City, MI

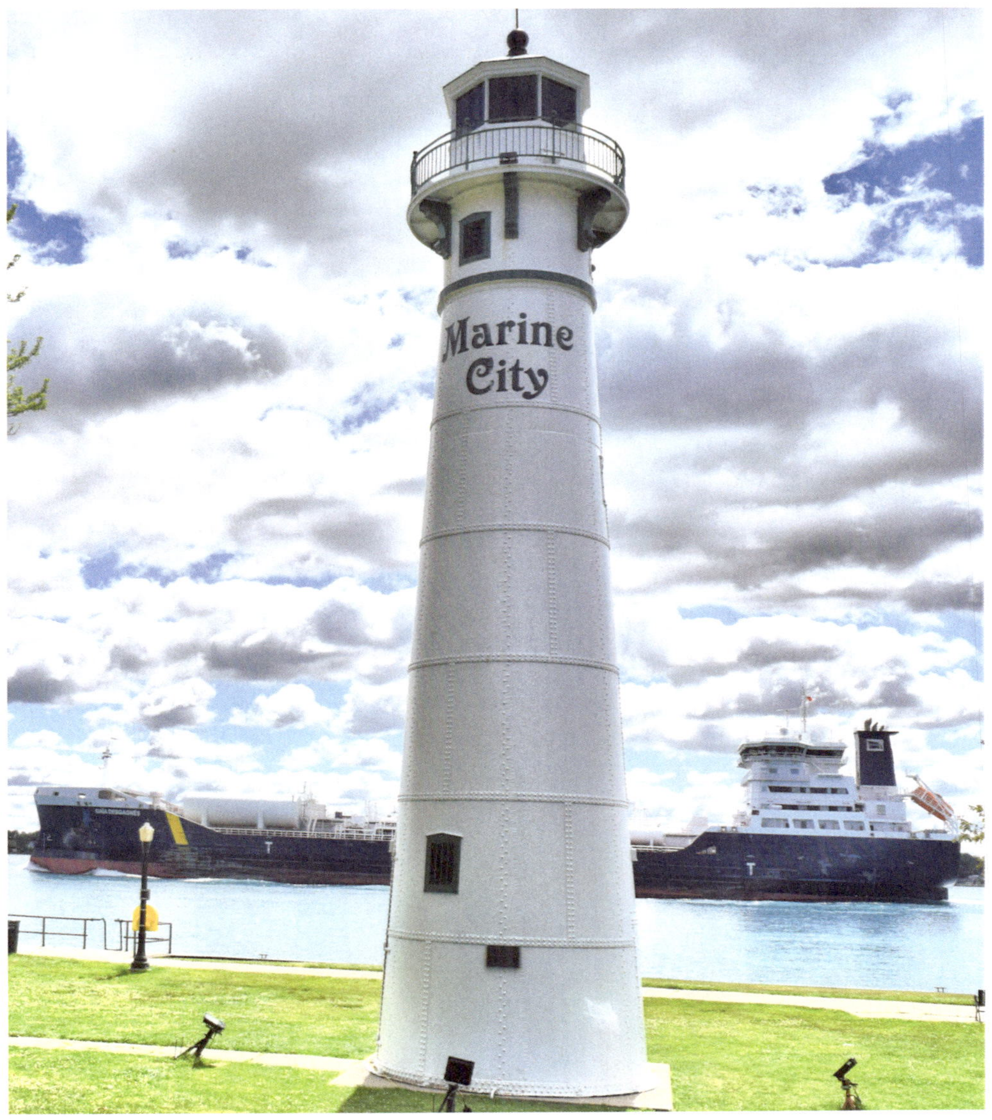

Constructed: 1908 - Located on the St. Clair River that connects Lake Huron and Lake Erie - Height: 38 feet

Lake Erie

Many of the lighthouses on Lake Erie are located at the end of piers or breakwaters, which were too dangerous to walk on. It was time to use my 600 mm lens to take the photo.

Cedar Point Lighthouse shares the peninsula with an amusement park. A campground circles the historical dwelling.

Unlike Lake Superior, the shoreline is lined with homes. I was surprised to discover field after field of grapes in the rural area. Westfield, where the Barcelona Lighthouse is located, is home of Welches Grape Juice/Jelly. Many of the vineyards have converted to wineries.

Interesting fact about the borders of Ohio, Pennsylvania and New York, when boundaries were being drawn each was given access to Lake Erie. Pennsylvania only has 45 miles of shoreline.

I spent a good part of an afternoon trying to find the lighthouses in Buffalo, NY. Most were pier or breakwater steal crib lights. When I did find the one stone tower, it is on Coast Guard property that was closed to the public.

Marblehead Point Lighthouse - Marblehead Peninsula, Ohio

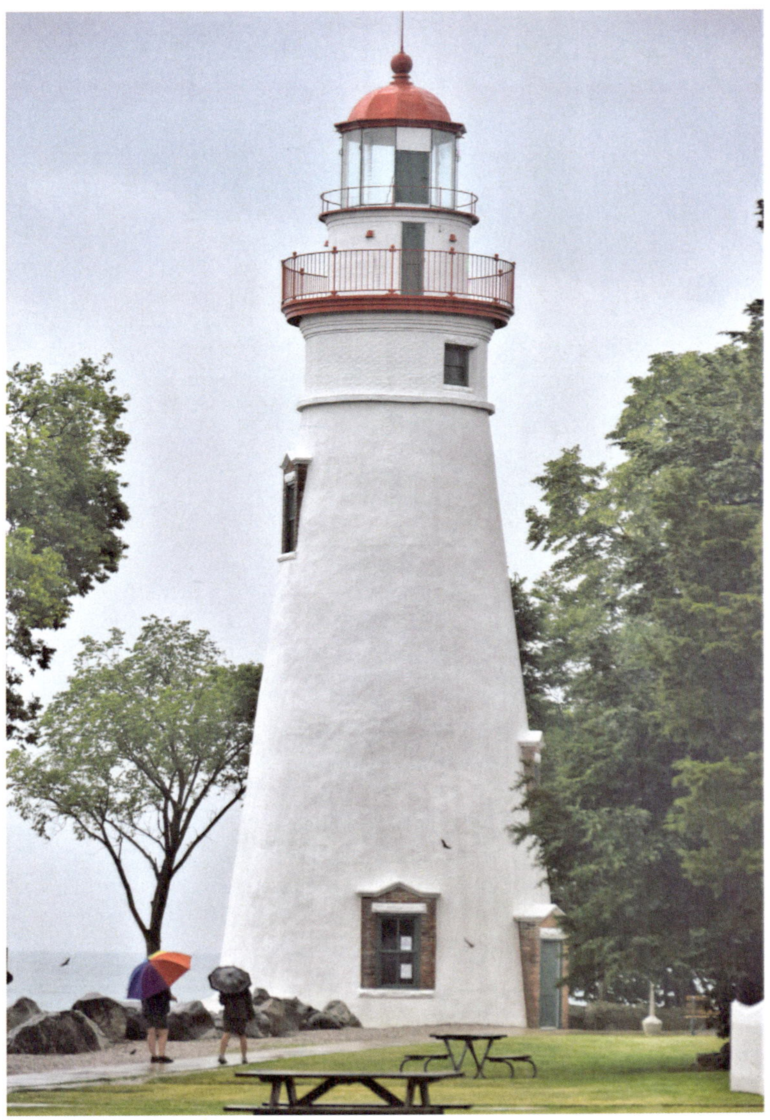

Constructed: 1821 - Light First Exhibited: June 1822 - Height: 65 feet
This is the oldest, continuously operated lighthouse on the Great Lakes. It appears on the Ohio license plate.

Cedar Point Lighthouse - Cedar Point, OH

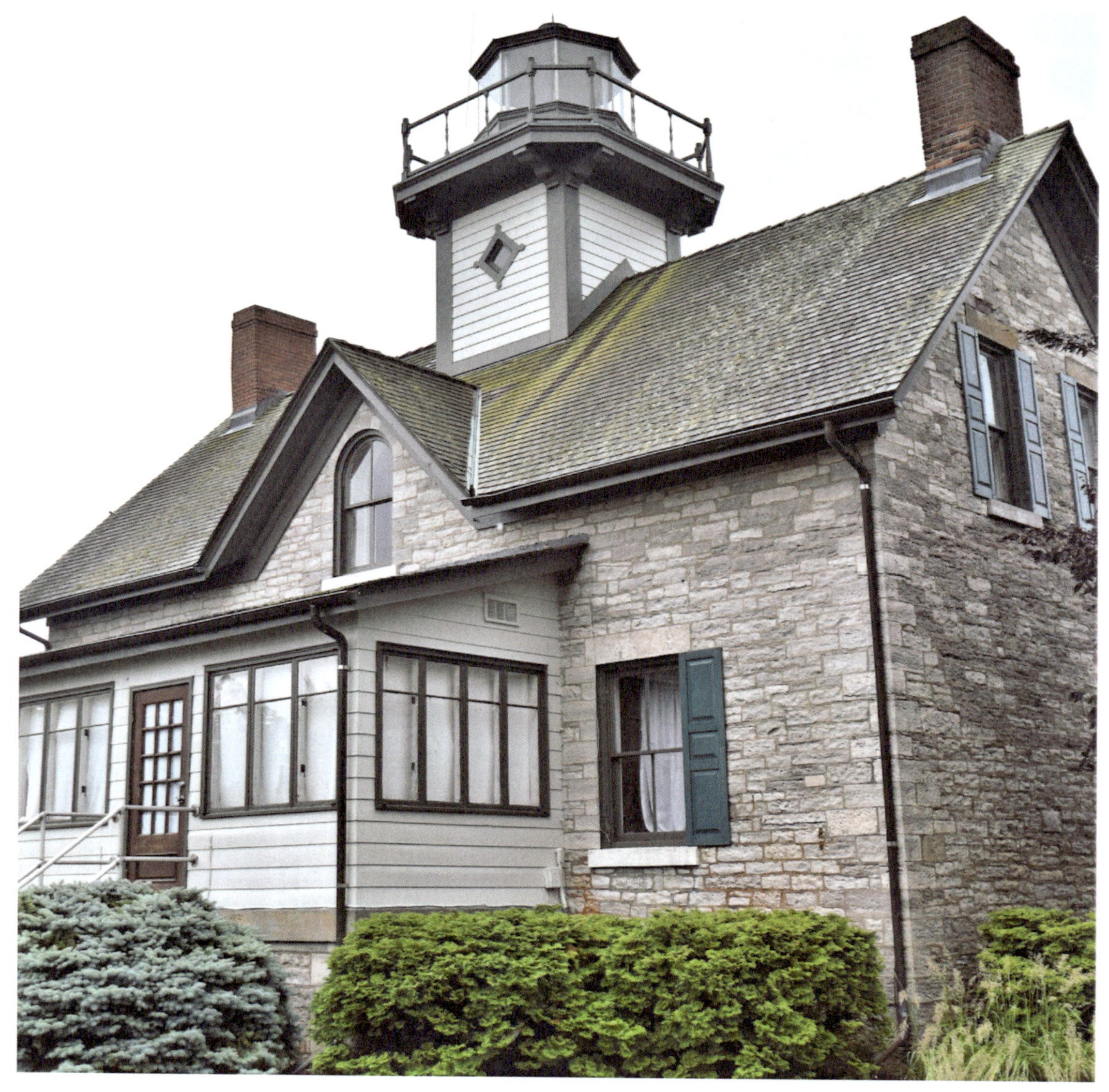

Constructed: 1862 - Light First Exhibited: 1862 - Height: 38 feet

Vermilion Lighthouse - Vermilion, OH

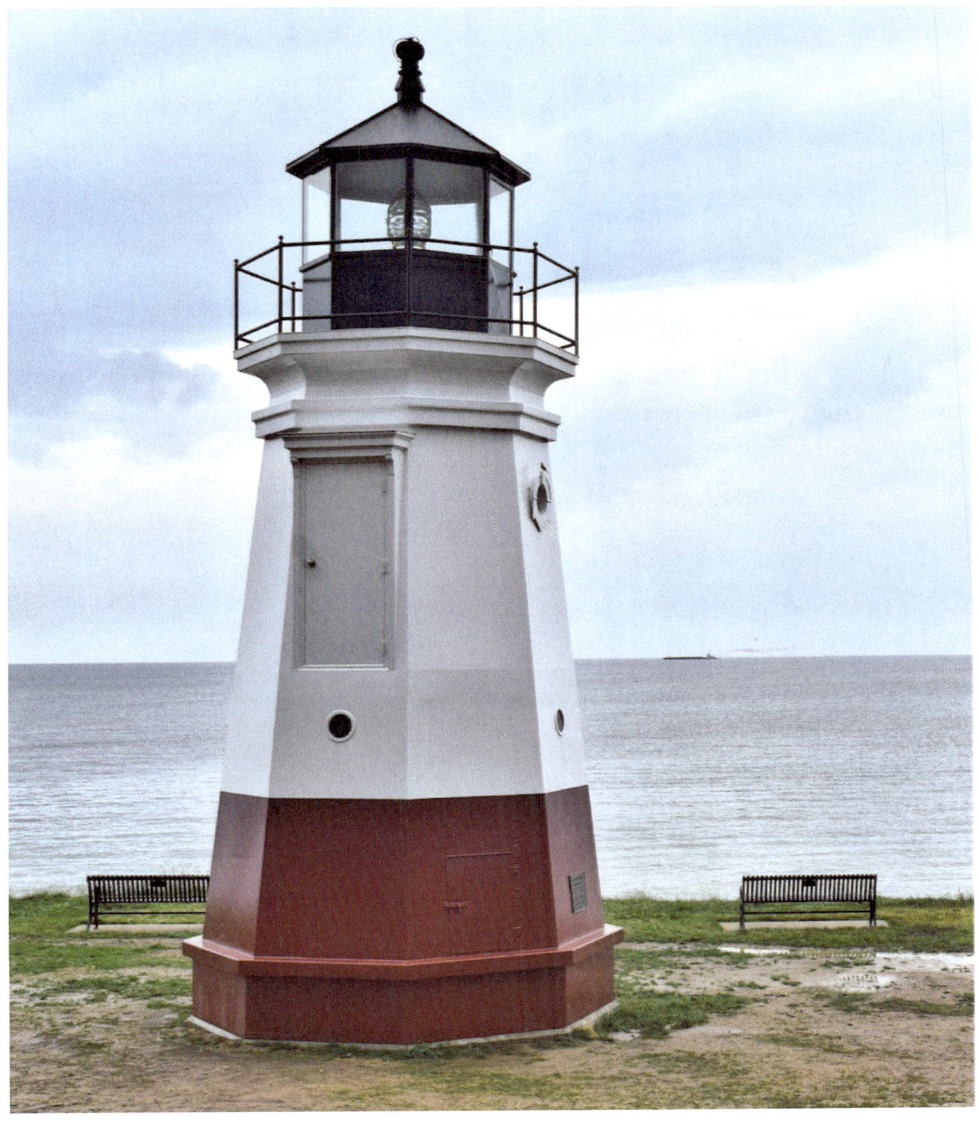

Construction: 1877 -Light First Exhibited: 1877 - Iron was from recycled Civil War cannons.

Lorain Point Lighthouse - Lorain, OH

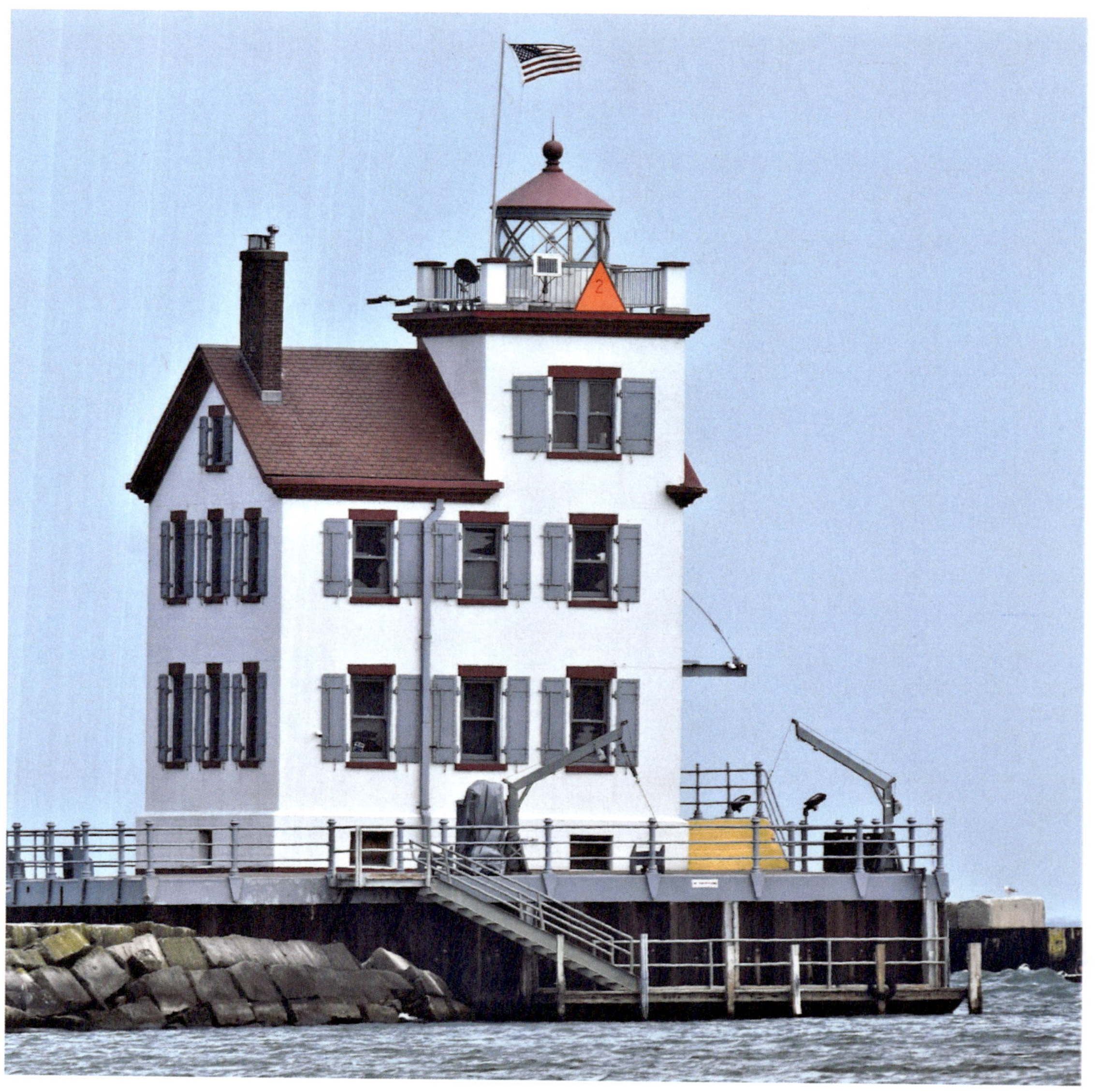

Constructed: 1919 - Light First Exhibited: April 1919 - Height: 51 feet

Cleveland Harbor West Pierhead Lighthouse - Cleveland, OH

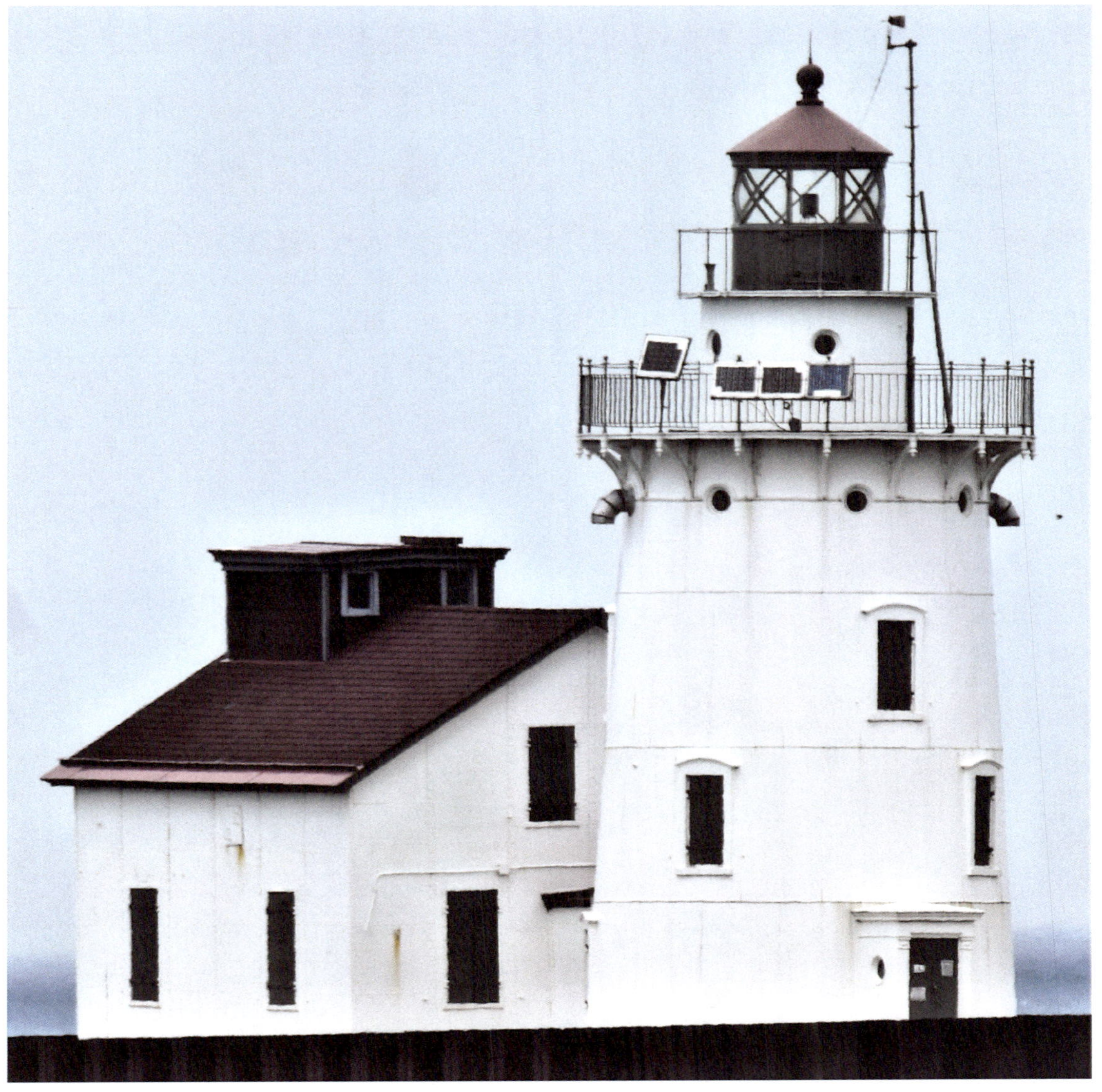

Constructed: 1911 - Light First Exhibited: March 1911 - Height: 25 feet

Fairport Harbor Lighthouse - Fairport, OH

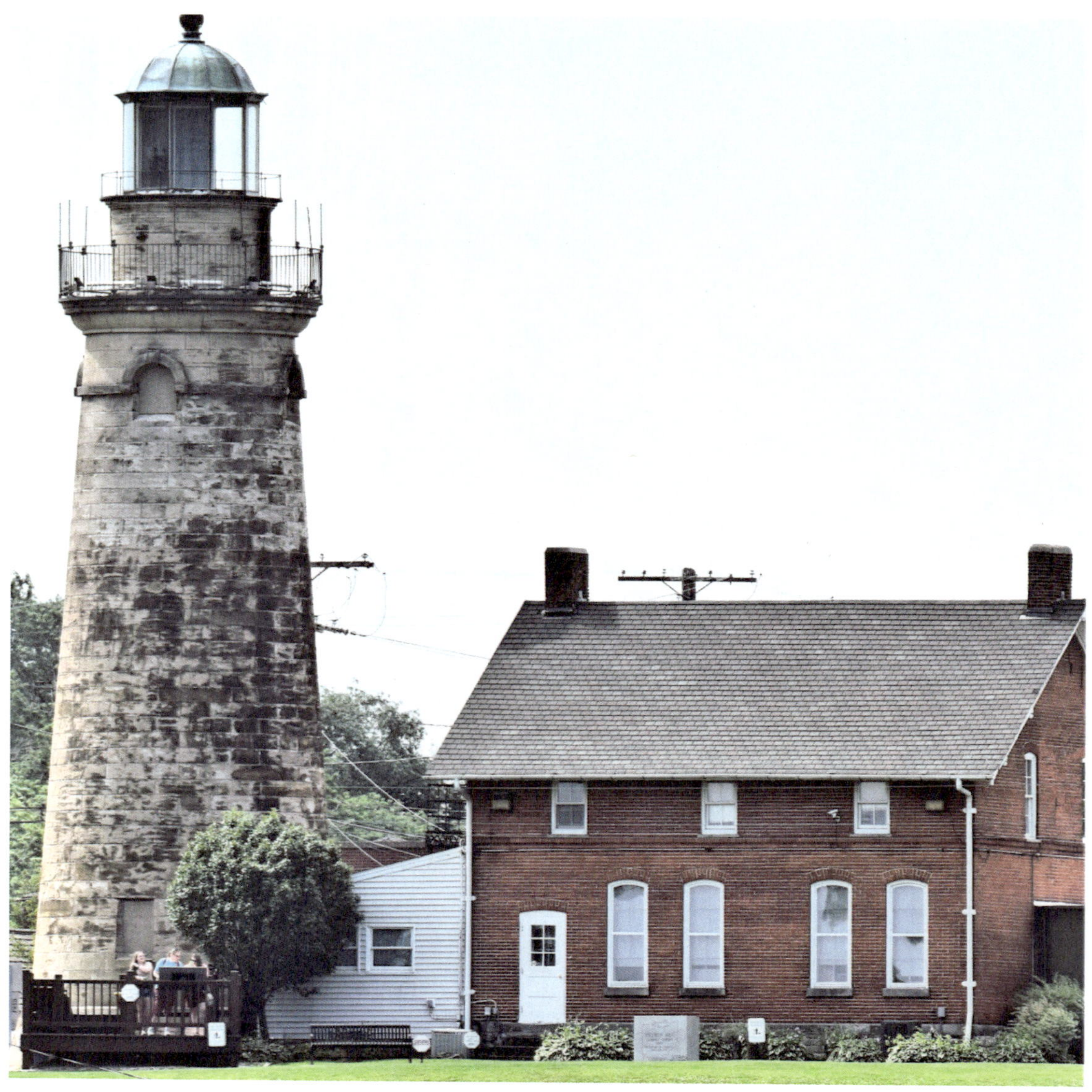

Constructed: 1825 - Light First Exhibited: 1825 - Height: 55 feet

Fairport Harbor West Breakwater Lighthouse - Fairport, OH

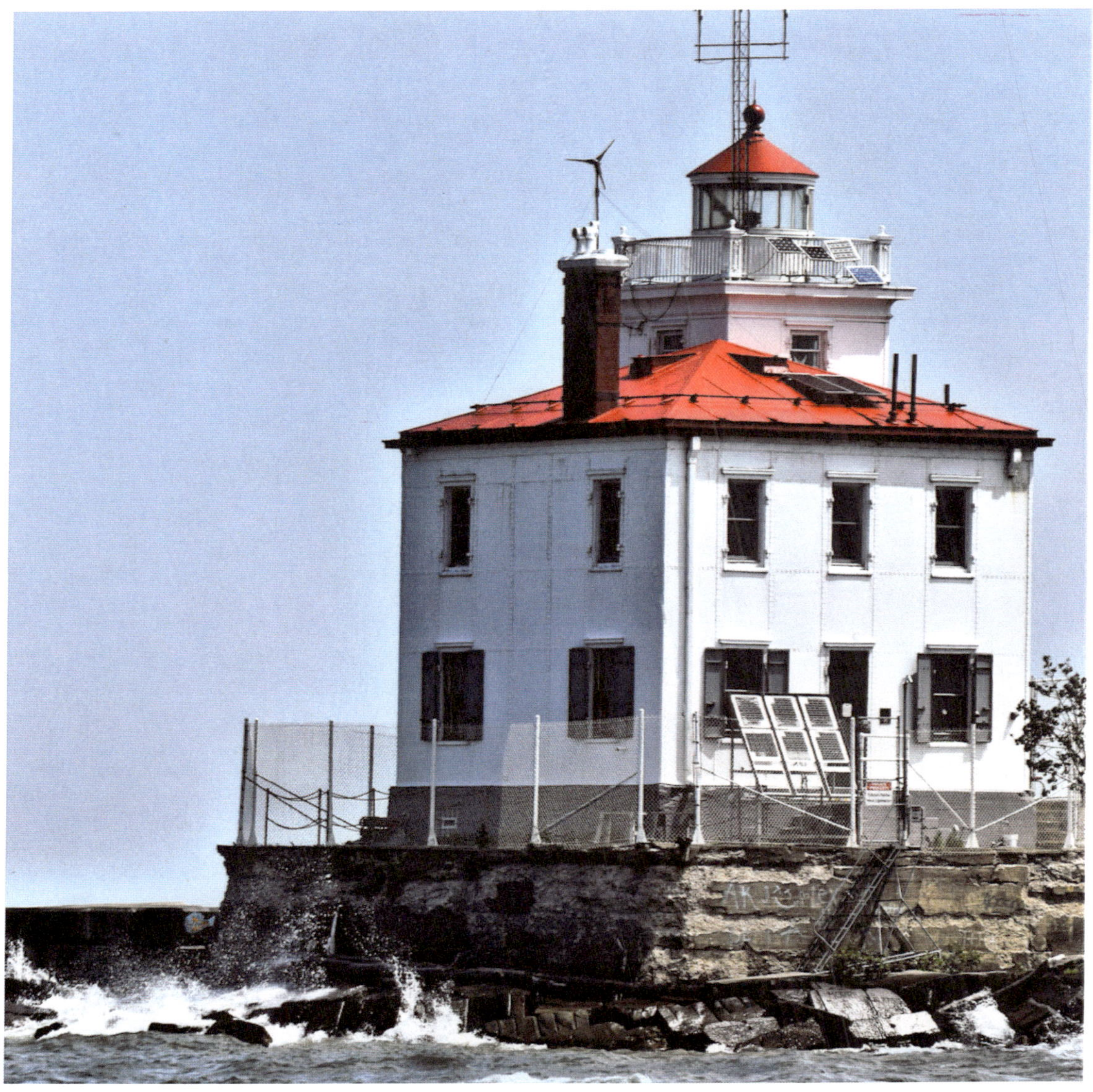

Constructed: 1920-24 - Light First Exhibited: June 1925 - Height: 38 feet

Presque Isle Lighthouse - Presque Isle, PA

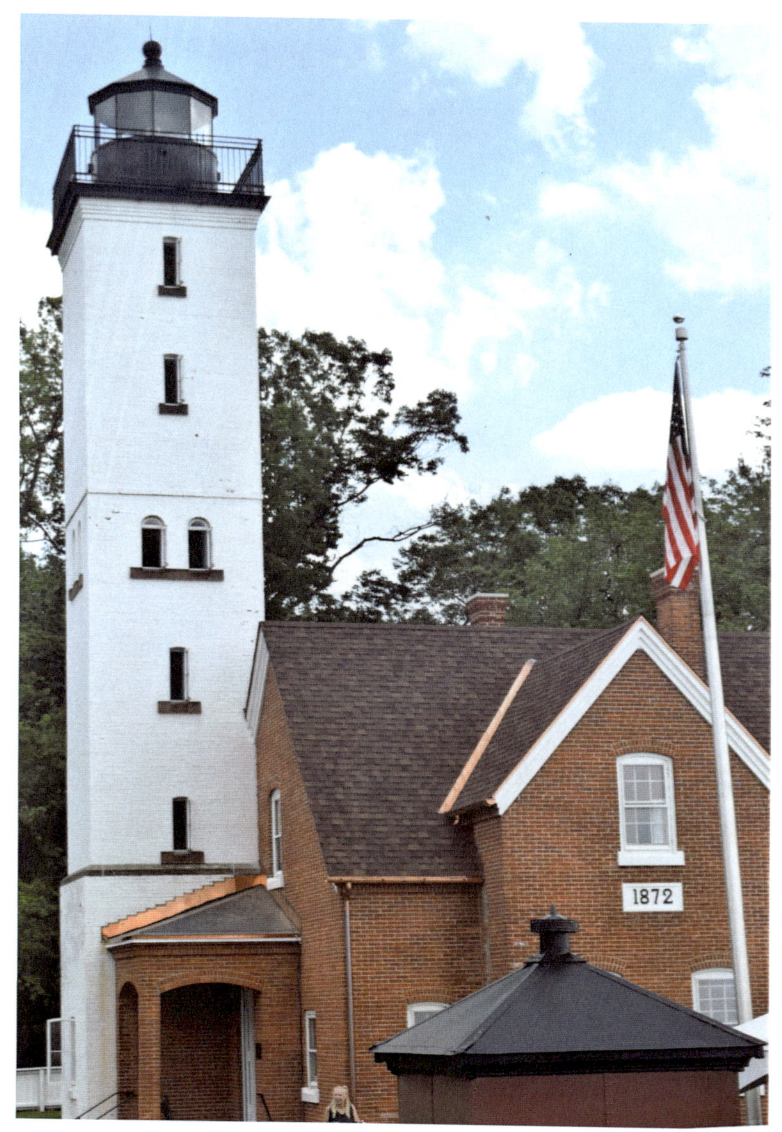

Constructed: 1872 - Light First Exhibited: July 1873 - Height: 68 feet

Erie Land Lighthouse - Erie, PA

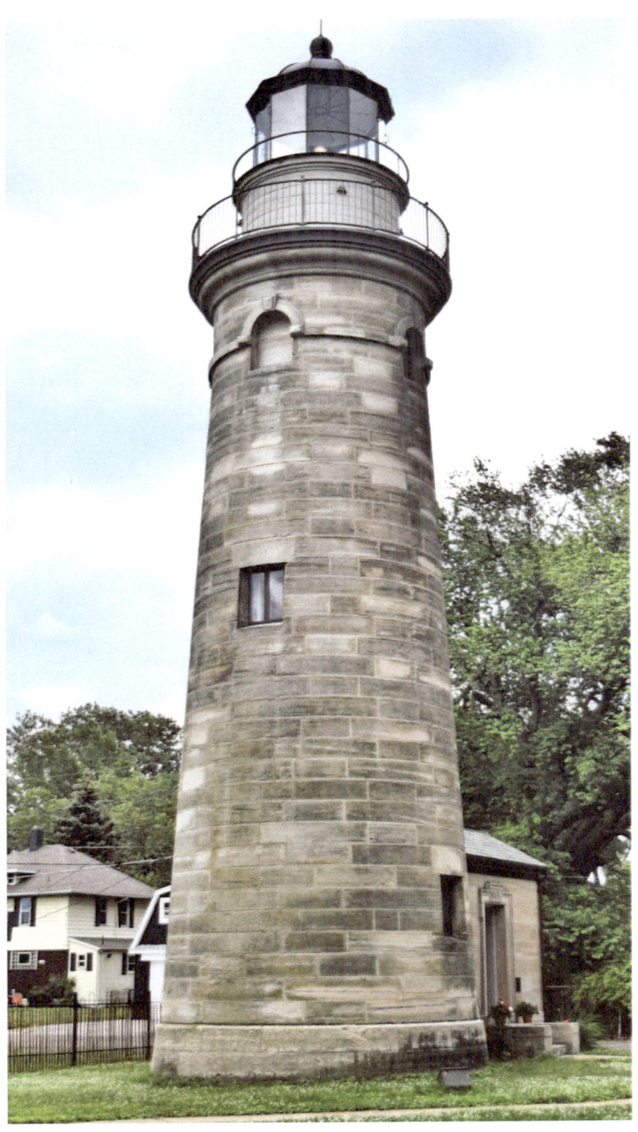

Constructed: 1867 - Light First Exhibited: 1868 - Height: 49 feet

Barcelona Lighthouse - Portland Harbor Westfield, NY

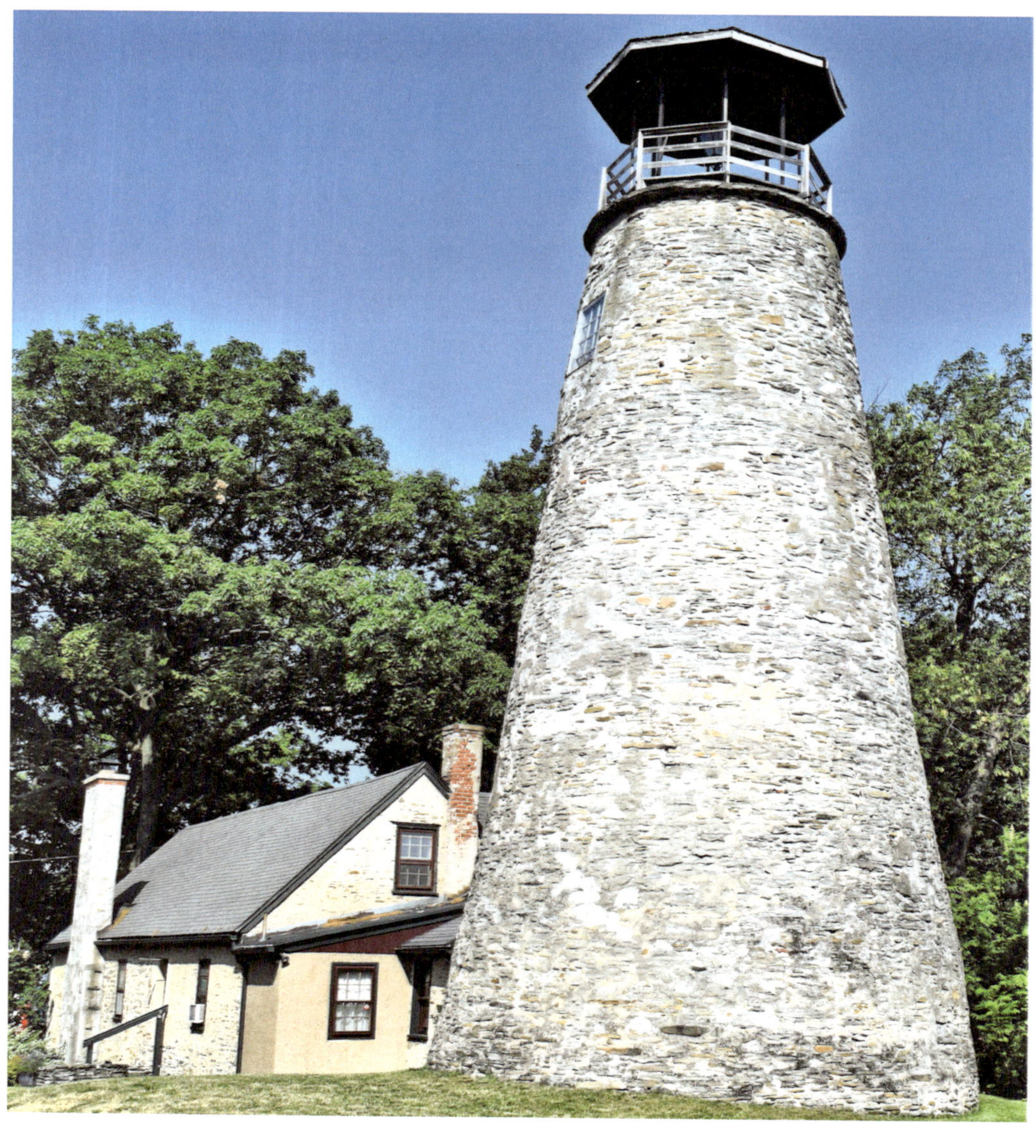

Constructed: 1828 - Light First Exhibited: 1829 - Height: 40 feet with a 22-foot diameter base

Dunkirk Lighthouse - Dunkirk, NY

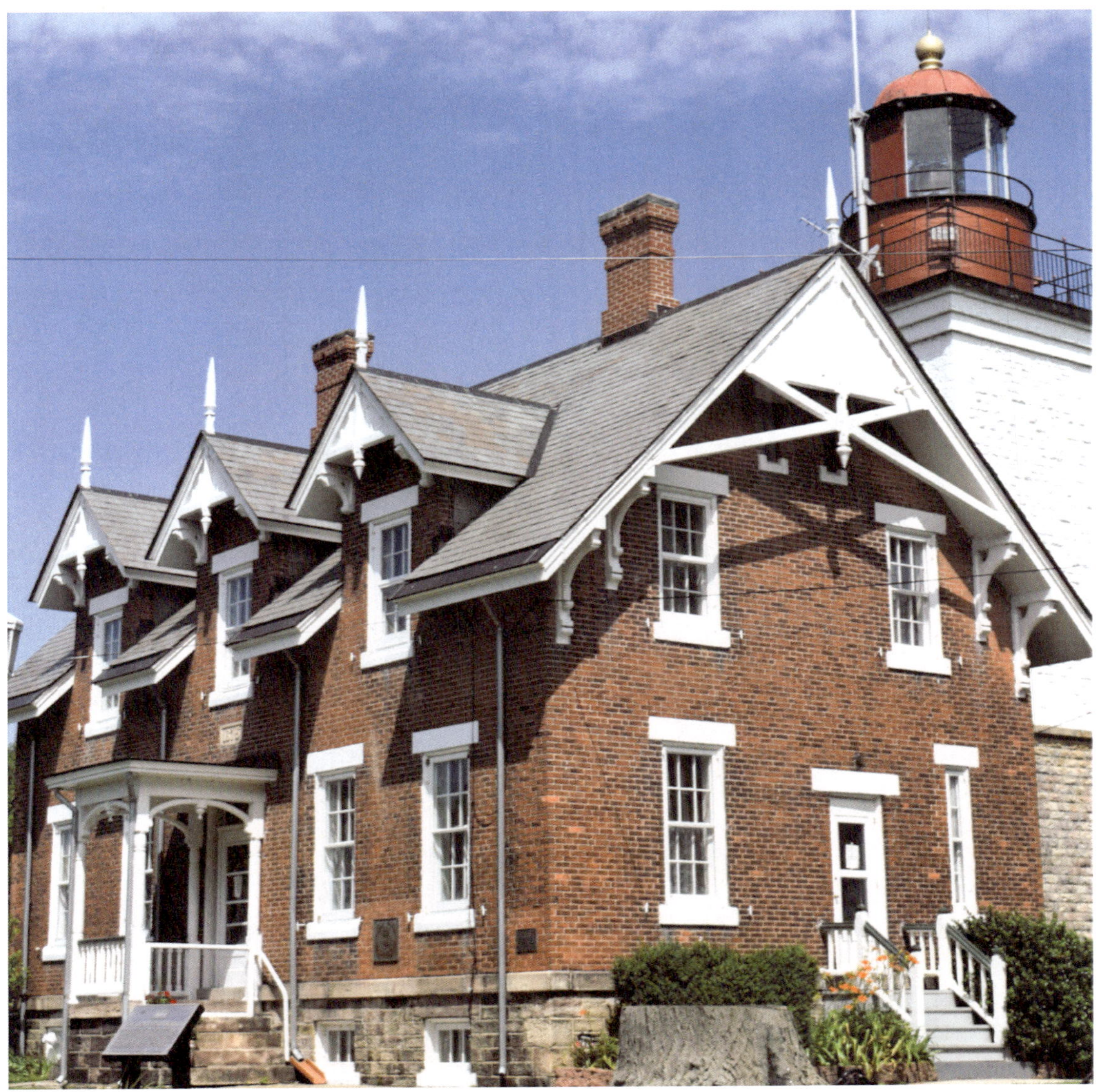

Construction: 1875 - Light First Exhibited: July 1876 - Height: 61 feet

Lake Ontario

The state of New York has secured shoreline of Lake Ontario for public-use with a series of state parks. Since I was in the area the weekend of the Fourth of July, the parks were overflowing with people enjoying access to the lake.

The first lighthouse I visited was Fort Niagara Lighthouse. The stonework on this tower and attached oil storage building is amazing. When the lantern galley needed to be raised, they used common bricks. While plain compared to the stonework, the builders added their own artist touch.

The Niagara River flows into Lake Ontario at the Old Fort location. Because of Niagara Falls, ships traveling between Lake Ontario and Lake Erie use the Welland Canal that is on the Canada side of the lakes.

Many of the lighthouses were the third generation building at the site, with the original facilities being built of wood and not surviving the harsh weather.

Sodus Point Lighthouse has the nicest landscaped grounds with colorful hydrangea bushes. Braddock Point Lighthouse has been called the prettiest dwelling building. The property was gated, so I had to view it from a distance.

Tibbetts Point Lighthouse is the last signal on Lake Ontario. The tower and fog horn building are perched on the 10-foot cliff overlooking the lake. It's Fresnel lens is one of 70 still in operation.

Fort Niagara Lighthouse

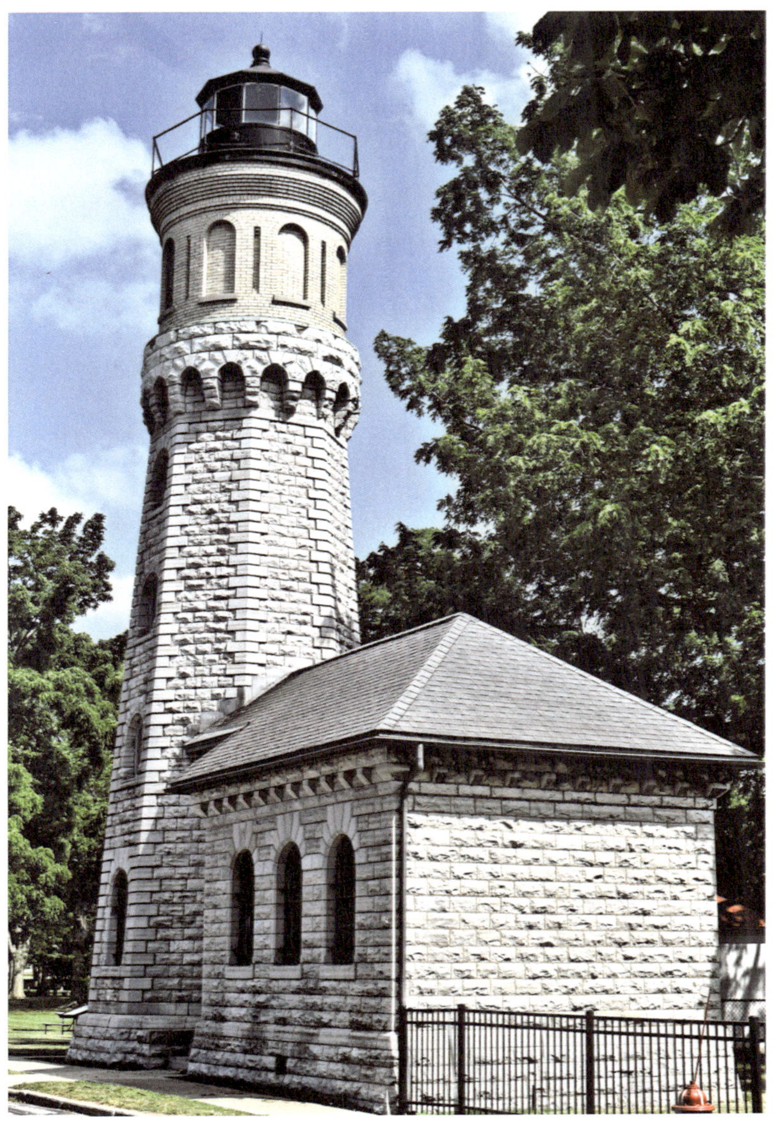

Constructed: 1872- Light First Exhibited: June 1872 - Height: 61-feet, 4-inches

Niagara-on-the-Lake, NY

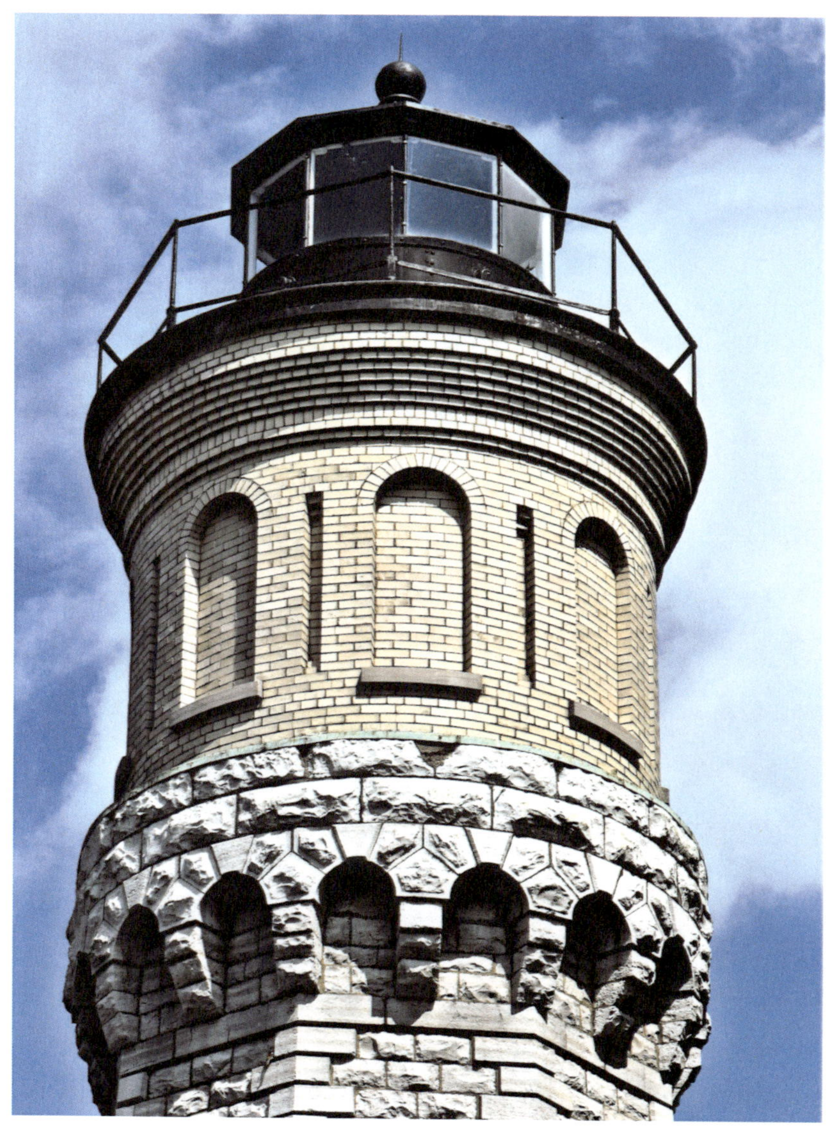

Original limestone tower was raised 11 feet, four inches in1900. Note the workmanship of the limestone.

Thirty Mile Point Lighthouse - Golden Hills State Park, NY

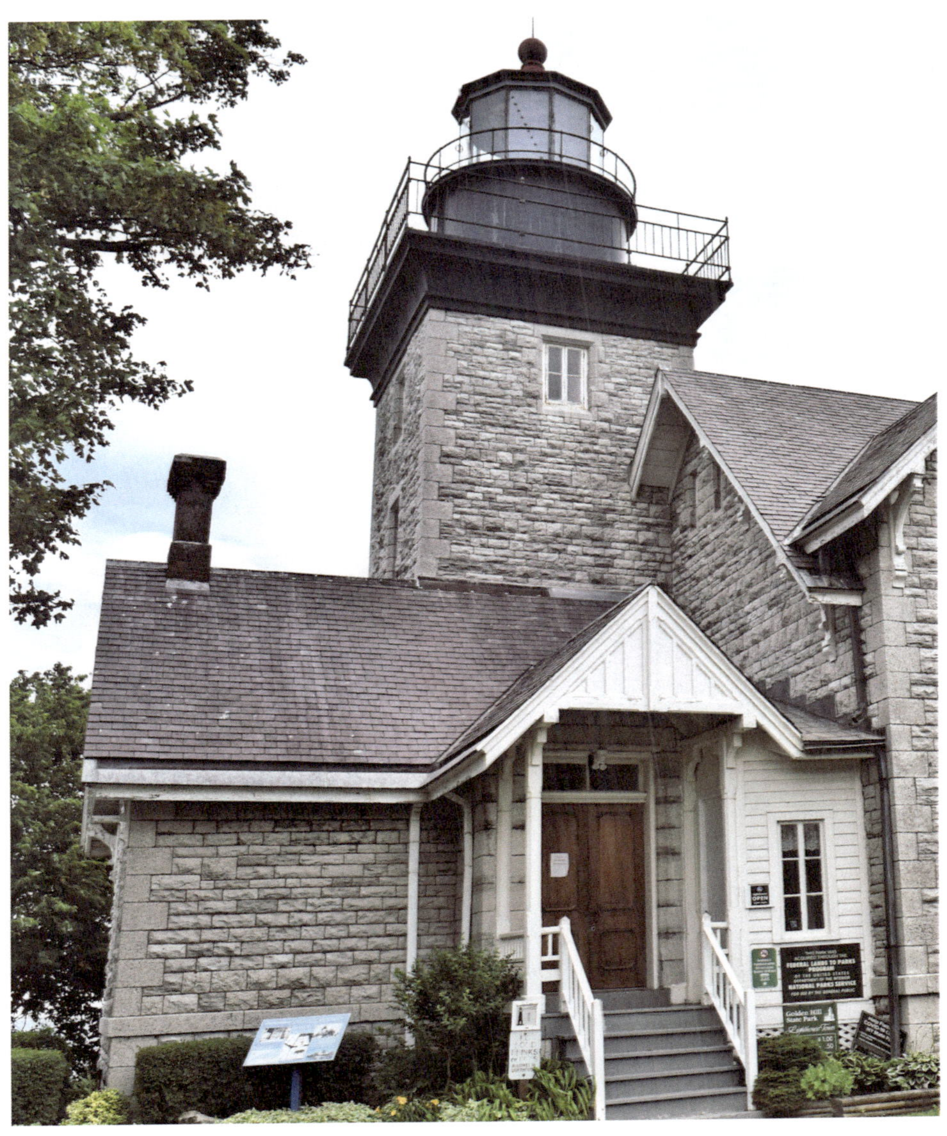

Constructed: 1876 - Light First Exhibited: April 1876- Height: 70 feet

Braddock Point Lighthouse - Bogus Point Hilton, NY

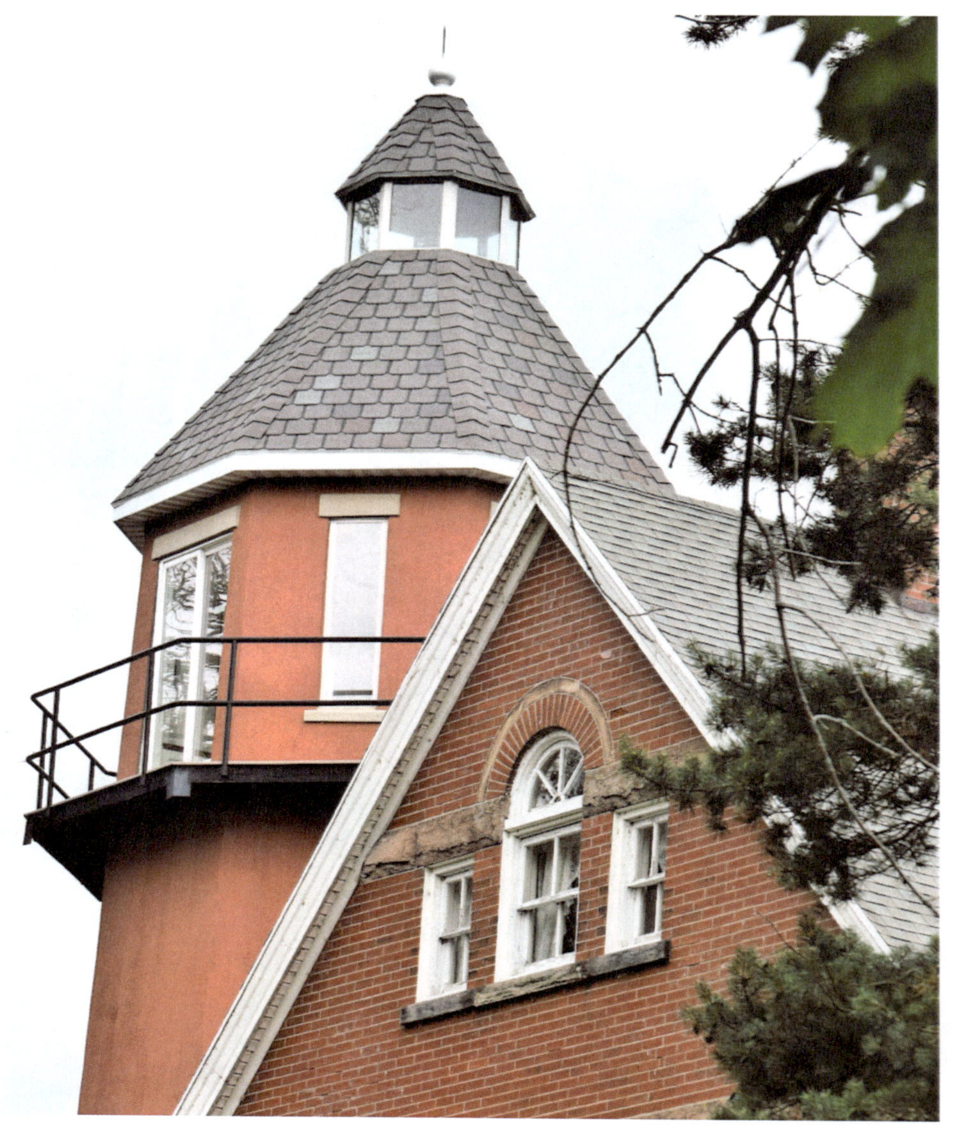

Constructed: 1895 - Light First Exhibited: August 1896 - Height: 97 feet

Charlott-Genesee Lighthouse - Rochester, NY

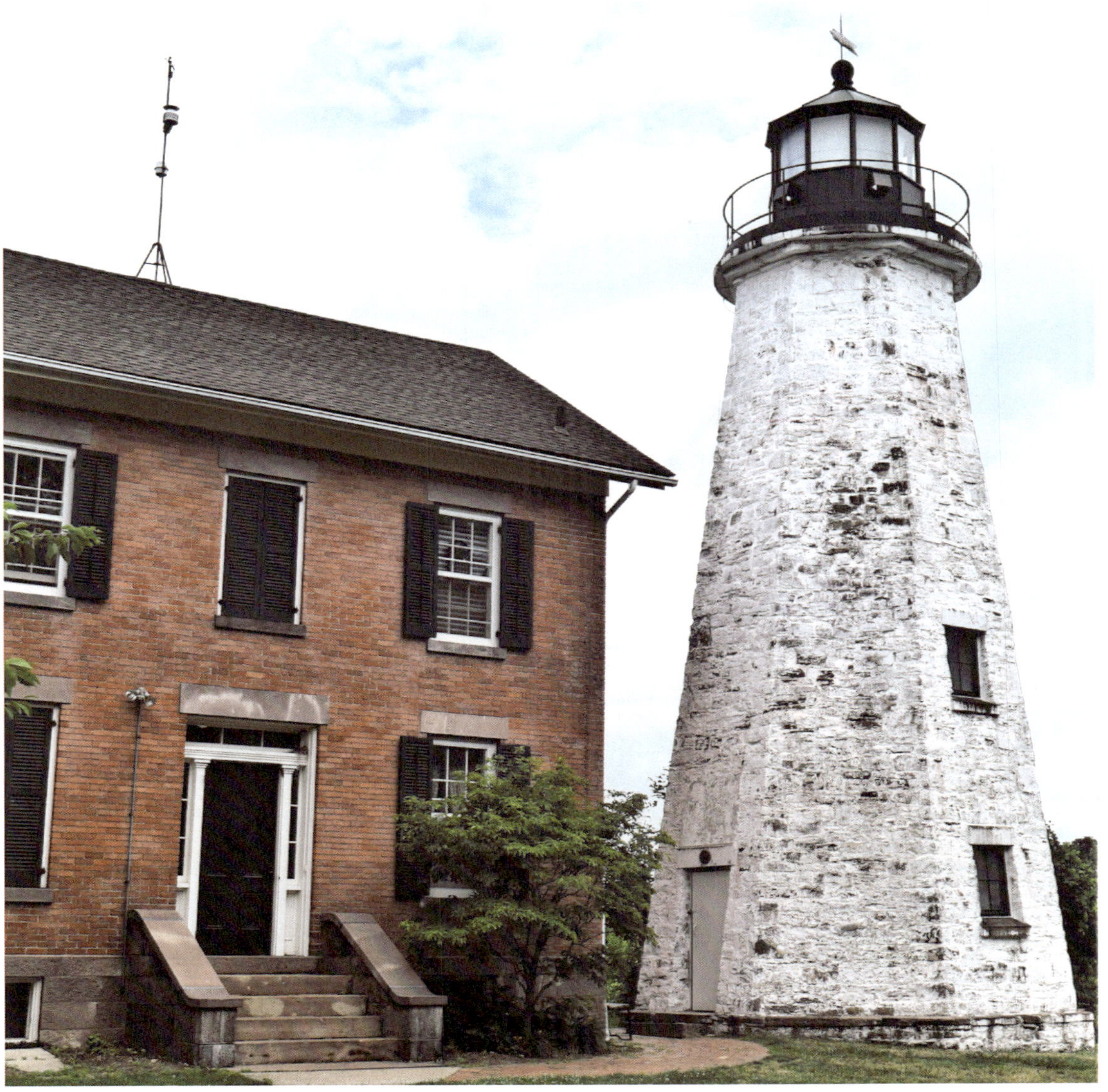

Constructed: 1822- Light First Exhibited: 1822 - Height: 44 feet

Sodus Point Lighthouse - Sodus Point, NY

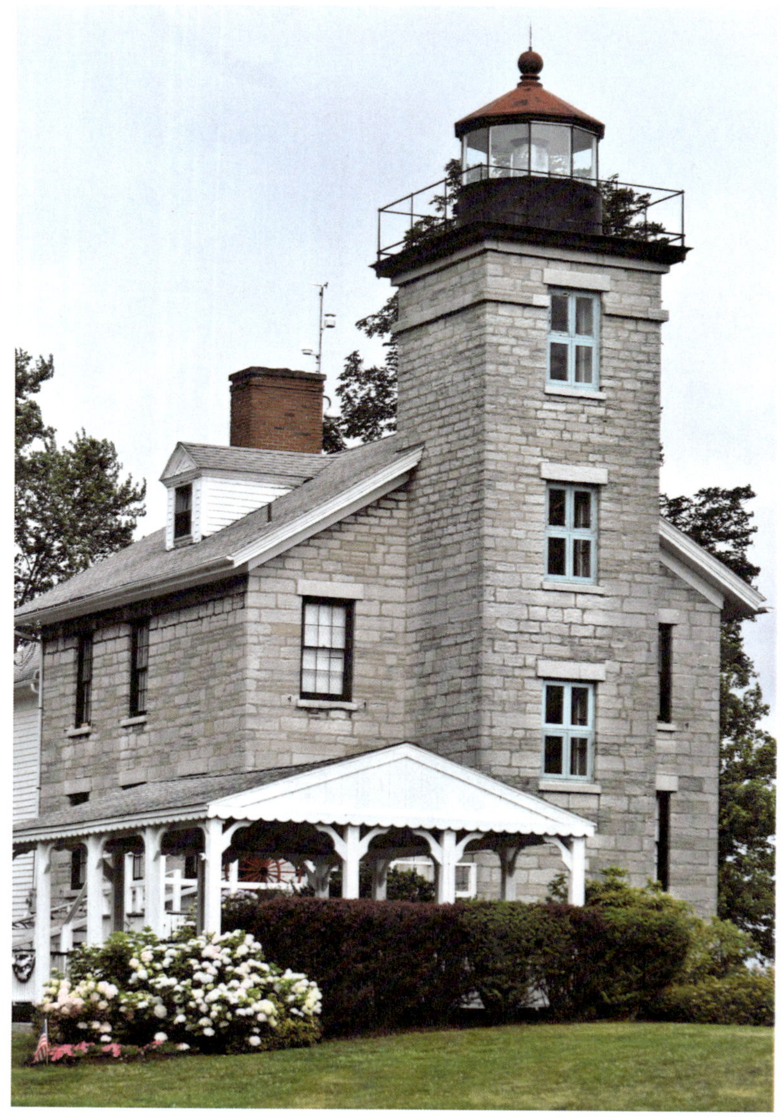

Constructed: 1871 - Light First Exhibited: 1871 - Height: 45 feet

Salmon River Lighthouse - Selkirk, NY

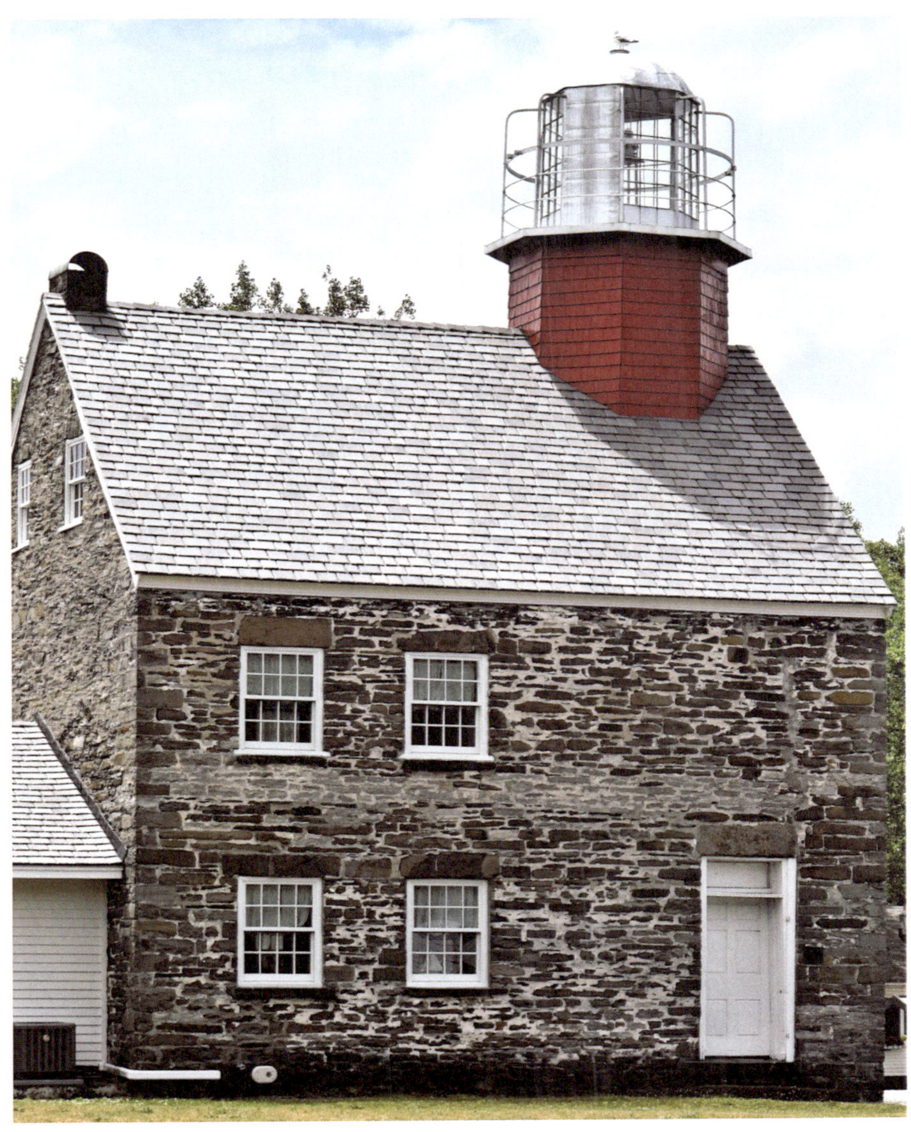

Constructed: 1838 - Light First Exhibited: 1838 - Height: 50 feet

Stony Point Lighthouse - Henderson Shores, NY

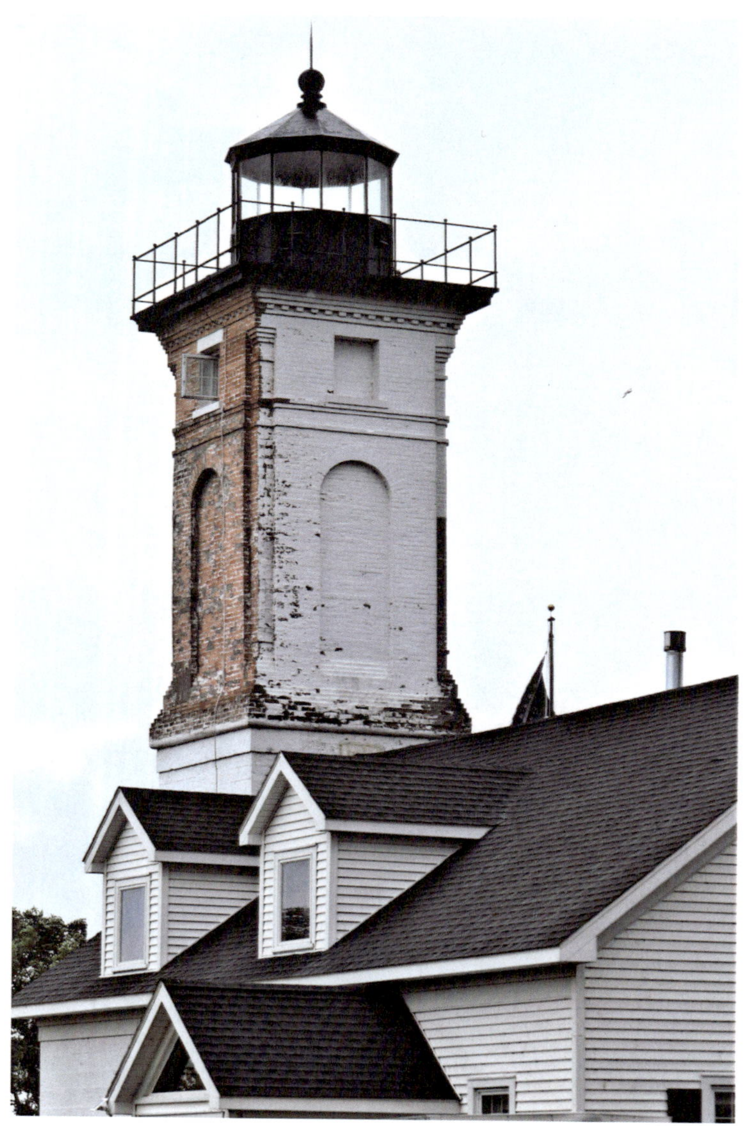

Constructed: 1869 - Light First Exhibited: 1869 - Height: 58 feet

Tibbetts Points Lighthouse - Tibbetts Point, NY

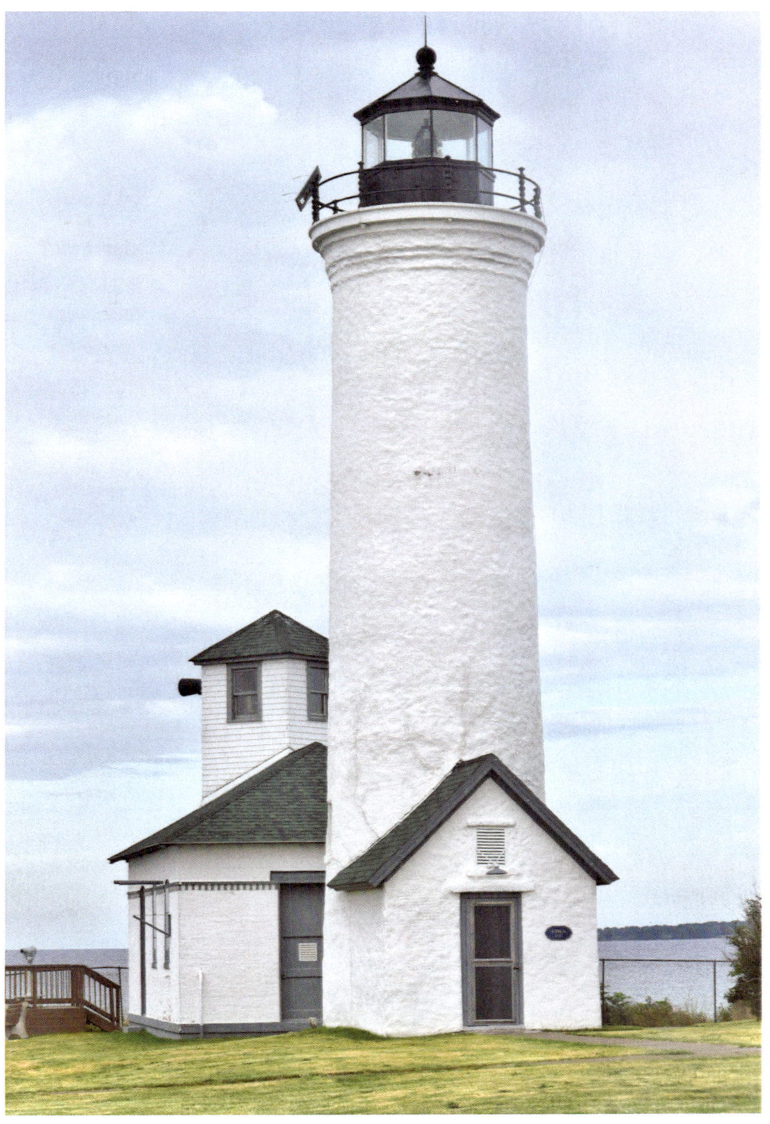

Constructed: 1827 - Light First Exhibited: 1827 - Height 30 feet

Thousand Islands St. Lawrence River

The Thousand Islands in the St. Lawrence River is a North American archipelago of 1,864 islands in a 50 mile stretch of the river. They range in size from 40 square miles to so small they are occupied by a single residence or are an uninhabited outcropping of rocks.

This was the playground for the rich and famous from New York City, Chicago, Cleveland and Pittsburg during the half century (1874-1912). Lavish homes were built on private islands including Singer Castle, owned by the president of Singer Sewing Machine Corporation.

The area has long been a center for recreational boating. The Antique Boat Museum, in Clayton, NY, displays its collection of boats from canoes to motor boats including racing speed boats.

Four of the lighthouses photographed were on islands, the largest being Rock Island Lighthouse. To get these photos, I had to find a view of the lighthouse, then ask the property owner if I could take the shot from their yard.

While photographing Rock Island Lighthouse a freighter passed between my location on Wellesley Island and Rock Island. It really put the size of ships in perspective.

The final lighthouse of the trip was Ogdensburg Harbor Lighthouse. This dwelling has been privately owned since World War II. I met the current resident, Blair Roethel. He grew up in the home and is proud to continue to maintain it.

Rock Island Lighthouse - Fishers Landing, NY

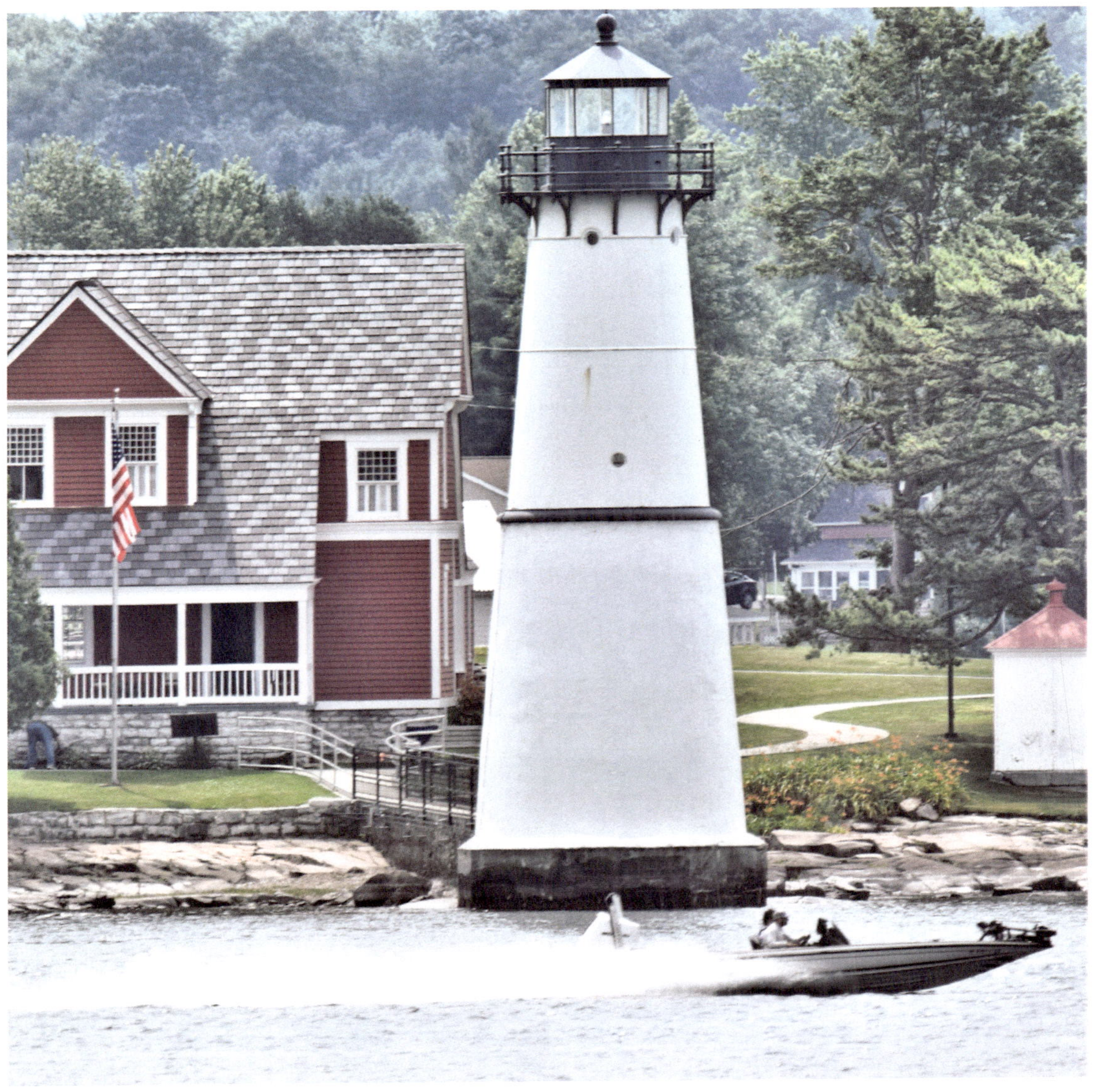

Constructed: 1884 - Light First Exhibited: 1884- Height: 50 feet

Sunken Rock Lighthouse - Thousand Islands, NY

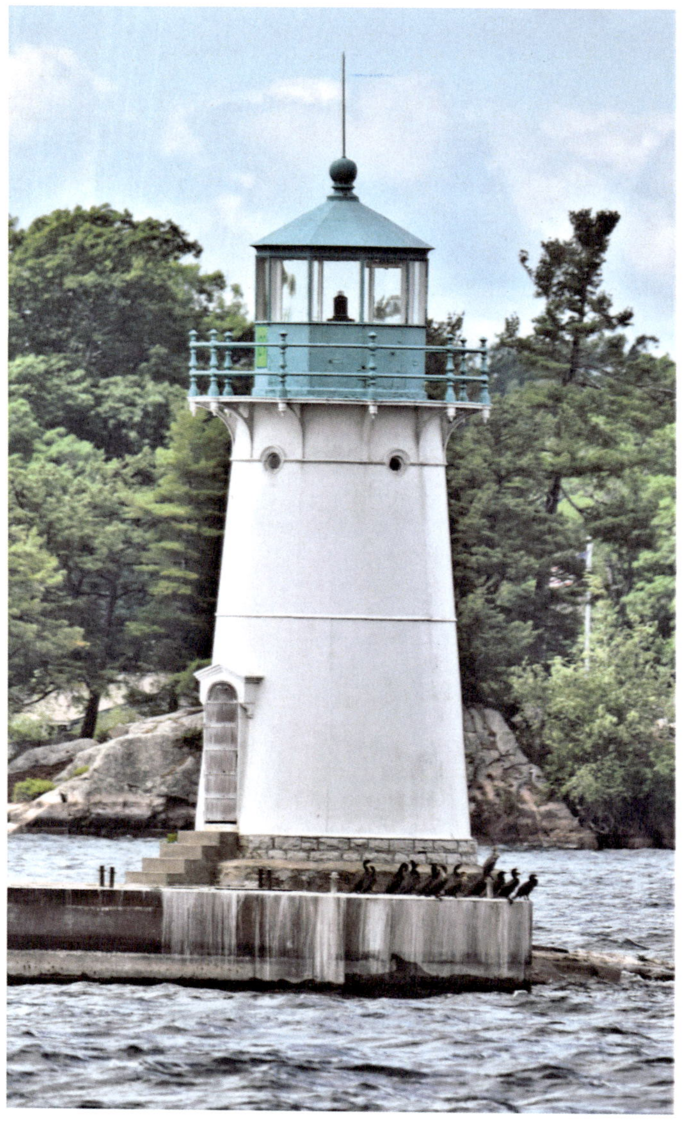

Constructed: 1882 - Light First Exhibited: June 1882 - Height: 30 feet

Crossover Island - Thousand Island, NY

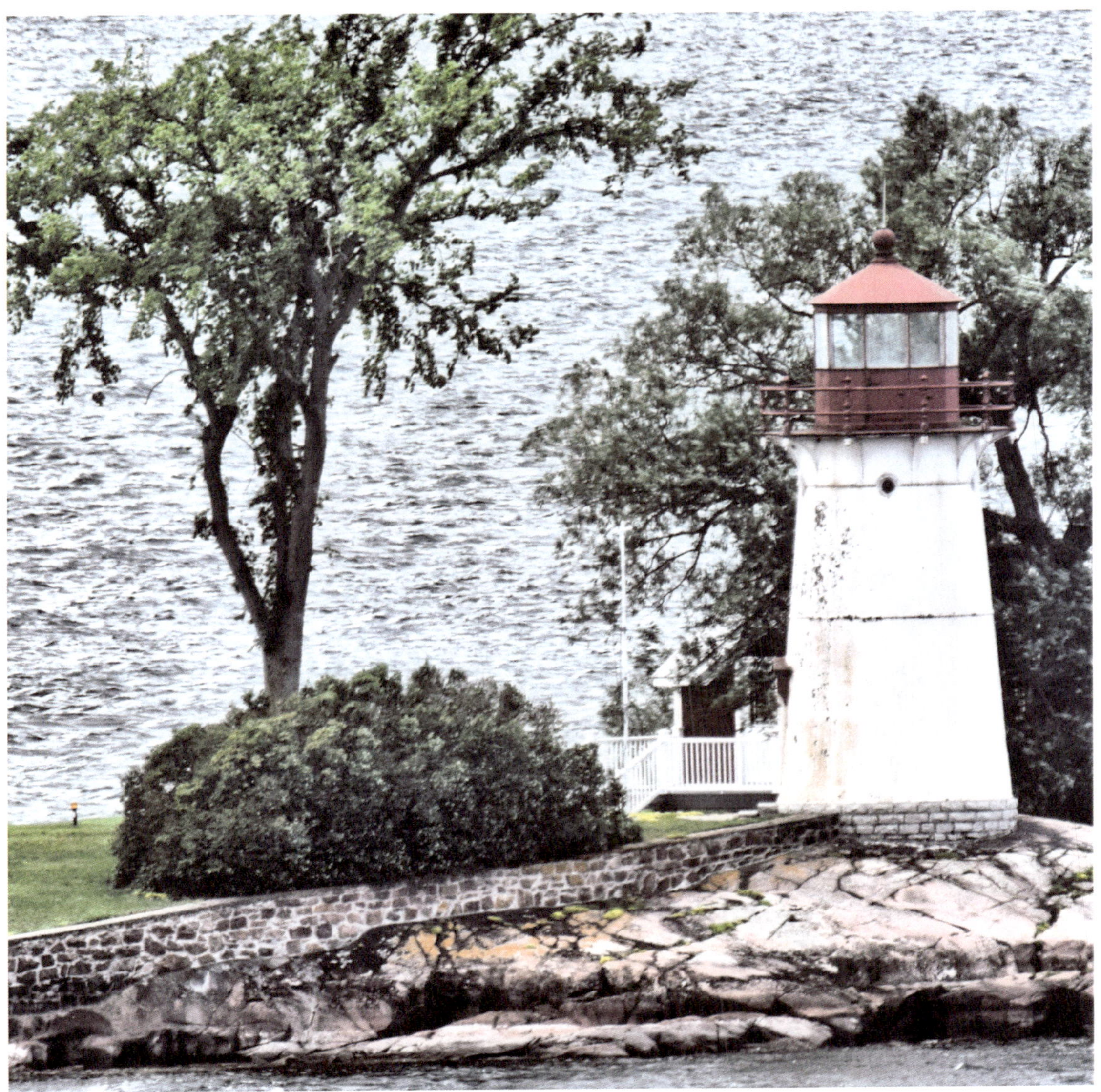

Constructed: 1882 - Light First Exhibited: 1882 - Height: 30 feet

Ogdensburg Harbor Lighthouse - Ogdensburg, NY

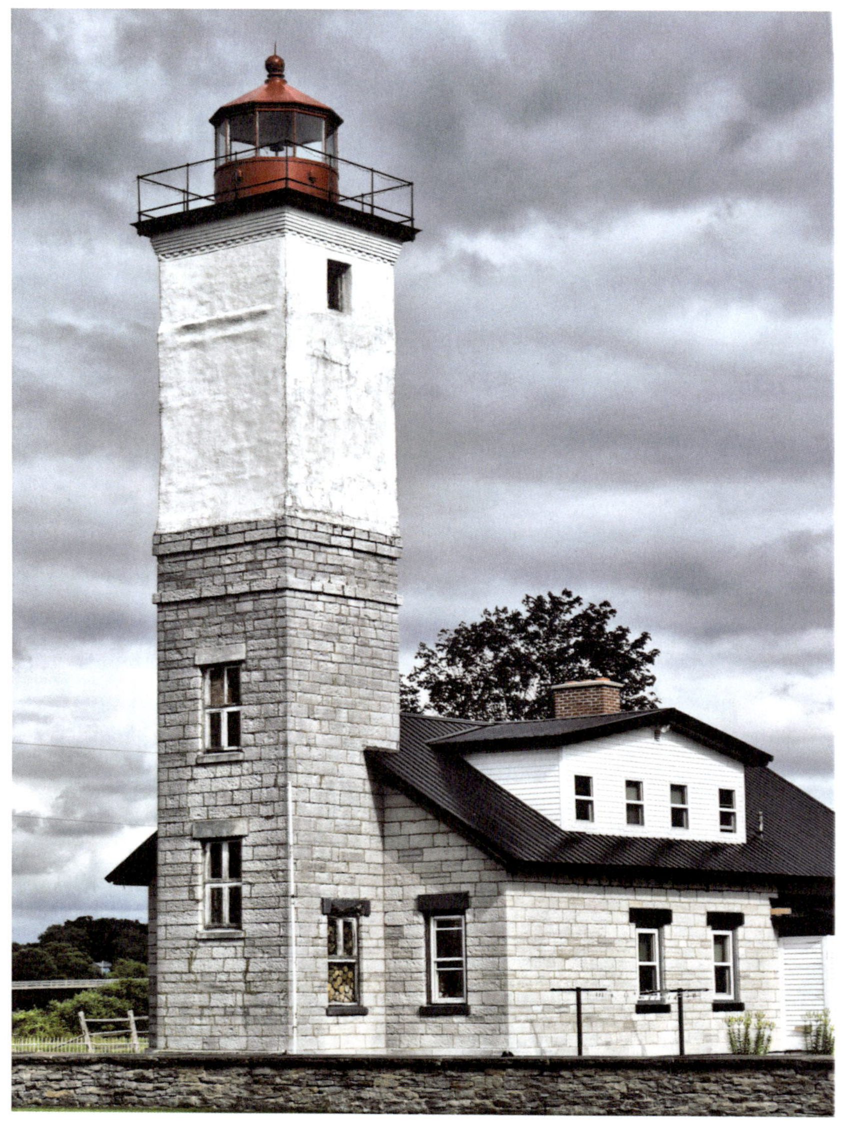

Construction: 1871 - Light First Exhibited: June 1871 - Height: 65 feet

About the Photographer

Jane Moorman describes herself as an adventurer who loves to drive the backroads to see what there is to see.

During her 30-year journalism career, Jane honed her photographic skills as a photojournalist including covering high school sporting events.

Upon retirement in 2021, her plans were to travel to Europe and "stay the summer." But the COVID-19 pandemic of 2020-21 kept her in the United States.

She decided there is a lot of her native country she had not seen, so until travel restrictions to Europe were lifted, she decided see the USA.

Jane currently lives in Albuquerque, New Mexico, but says her real home is on the road.

www.ingramcontent.com/pod-product-compliance
Lightning Source LLC
Chambersburg PA
CBRC090746110726
48005CB00008B/979